# Find the Hidden Treasures: A Guide to Mountain Bike Trails in Kananaskis Country

Peter Oprsal, creator of bikepirate.com

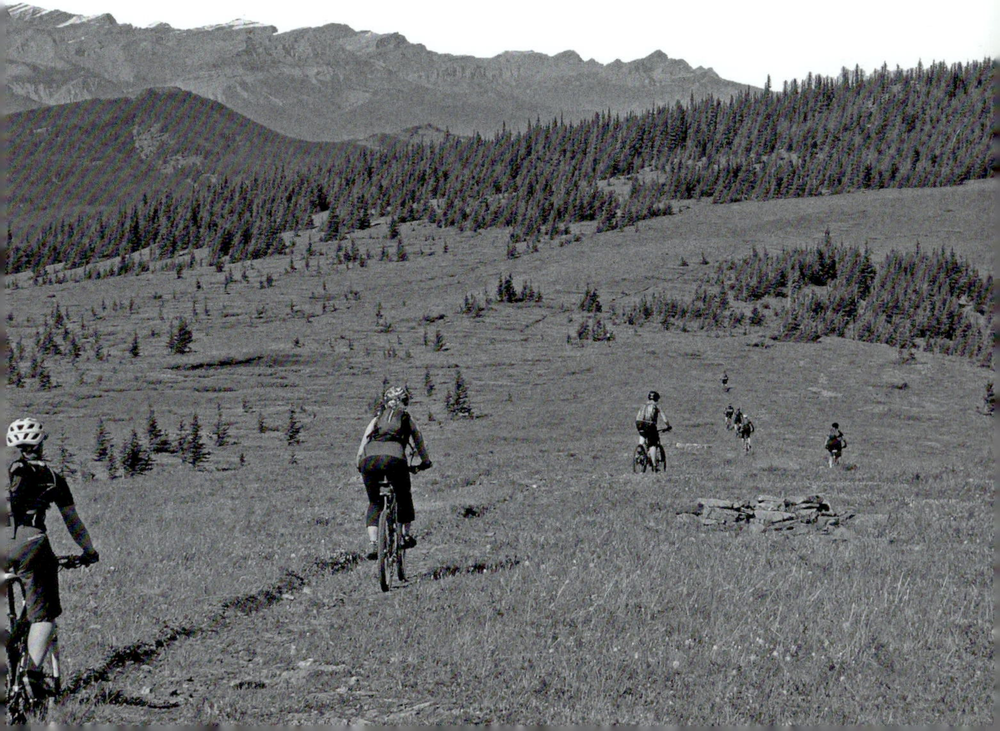

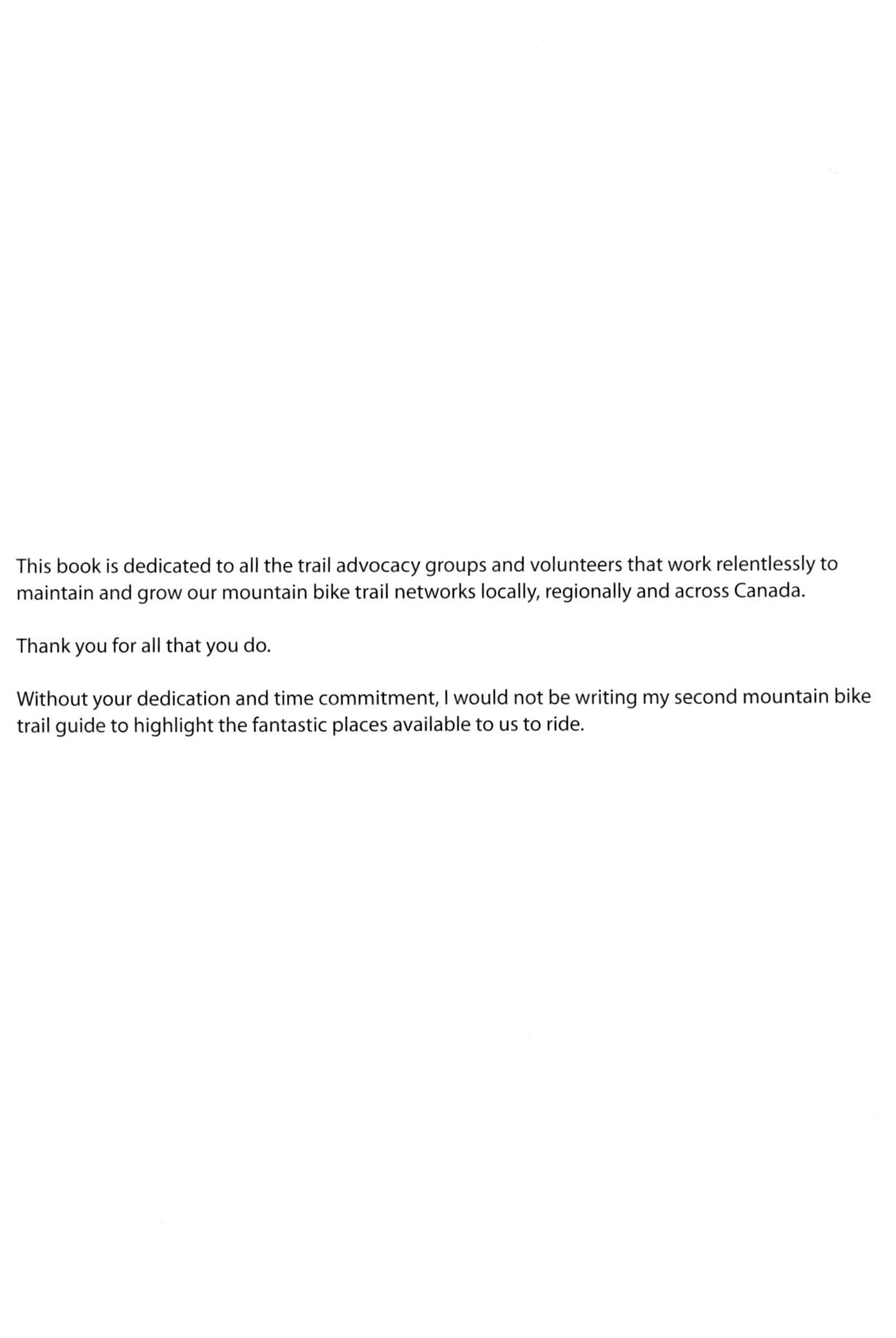

This book is dedicated to all the trail advocacy groups and volunteers that work relentlessly to maintain and grow our mountain bike trail networks locally, regionally and across Canada.

Thank you for all that you do.

Without your dedication and time commitment, I would not be writing my second mountain bike trail guide to highlight the fantastic places available to us to ride.

# DISCLAIMER

**Warning: Mountain biking has many inherent risks and dangers.** There are obstacles and hazards on every trail. These trails are not patrolled and conditions may change quickly. Communicating for any reason can be difficult and help may be hours away or unavailable. The user of this book agrees to use the guidebook at their own risk and agrees to waive any and all claims against its creators and bikepirate.com from any liability for any loss, damage, expense, or injury (including death) sustained by the guidebook user as a result of cycling the trails listed in this book.

**This guidebook is not a substitute for experience and proper judgement.** The authors, publishers, and distributors of this book do not recognize any liability for injury or damage caused to, or by, hikers, mountain bikers, third parties or property arising from such persons seeking reliance on this guidebook as an assurance of their own safety. Your use of this book indicates your assumption of the risk that it may contain errors and is an acknowledgement of your own sole responsibility for your safety.

1st edition – April 2013

© 2013 Peter Oprsal (author and creator of bikepirate.com - info@bikepirate.com)

© 2013 Peter Oprsal (photography). All photos taken by Peter Oprsal, unless otherwise indicated.

Design by Peter Oprsal

Copy editing by Joanna Cockerline (joanna.cockerline@shaw.ca)

Printed and bound in Canada by Friesens

International Standard Book Number | ISBN 978-0-9879343-2-1

## MAPS



## ADVERTISERS

Mountain biking has come a long way since the heady days of the nineteen eighties when Gerhart Lepp cycled many of the hiking trails in the Canadian Rockies and then wrote them up in a trail guide called Backcountry Biking in the Canadian Rockies.  In the years since then, bicycle technology has changed in amazing and wonderful ways to make the machines more capable than ever.  As the bikes evolved so did the desires and dreams of the people who ride them. Today we sometimes use the machine as a sort of iron horse to cover epic distances across the landscape, sometimes for exercise or for an enjoyable social outing; other times we use our bikes to demonstrate amazing feats of technical riding prowess.  The fundamental need in all of this is, of course, the trails on which we ride. Finding suitable trails is key to an enjoyable experience.

Today the range of trails being cycled in the Rockies varies from the old school hiking trails that have existed for years to the rider-built new school trails that cater specifically to the technical aspects of all-mountain and downhill riding.  With this evolution of the sport comes the need for a trail guide that reflects these new realities.  This volume represents the next step in guidebook evolution and focuses on one of the best riding areas in the Canadian Rockies.  Here Peter Oprsal shows us the current offer of cycling opportunities available on the eastern slopes located to the west of Calgary in Kananaskis Country.  This guidebook features a combination of new school all-mountain and downhill trails as well as many of the old favourite shared use trails that lead to exciting backcountry destinations.

Although mountain biking is frequently about speed and fast-paced fun, I feel a need to remind you to take some time to smell the roses along the way.  These trails will lead you through some of the most spectacular country in the Rockies and rushing through it at high speed will reduce your trail time to little more than the experience you would get from riding on a set of rollers.  The best advice I can give you is to use your bike as a means to get in touch with the amazing natural world values of the eastern slopes.  As you ride, always be receptive to that magic moment when human, machine, trail and natural world blend together into a single perfect experience.  It is this sometimes elusive zen-like experience that draws us back to mountain biking time after time.

Happy trails.

Doug Eastcott

This book would not be possible without the incredible support I've received, but more importantly without the efforts of key trail advocacy groups, not-for-profit organizations and the volunteers who spend countless hours working to maintain and build trails for all of us to enjoy. A big thank you goes out to all of you - you know who you are - and to the Moose Mountain Bike Trail Society, Greater Bragg Creek Trails Association, Friends of Kananaskis Country, Bow Valley Mountain Bike Alliance and Calgary Mountain Bike Alliance for their dedication, time and effort spent to keep our trails maintained and open for all to enjoy.

A special thank you to the following individuals who supported my efforts in writing this book, providing me with key information to ensure the accuracy of the trails listed. Don Hill, Reg Mullett, David Barcham, Eric Lloyd, Duane Fizor, Scott Jevons, and Claude Faerden, your support throughout this process was truly appreciated. Also, a huge thank you goes out to Joanna Cockerline, the copy editor for this book and for my first book, Bow Valley Mountain Bike Trail Guide. Joanna has once again done a fantastic job of polishing up my work, adding clarity and consistency.

Thank you to Corrine Harris, my number one supporter. You are an incredible woman and your tremendous love and support throughout the process of creating this guidebook has been unwavering. Thank you for allowing me to follow my dreams and for supporting not only the books I write, but the work I do to grow bikepirate.com.

Over the last two years I've had the pleasure of getting to know and riding with Doug Eastcott, the author of the celebrated Backcountry Biking in the Canadian Rockies book. Although the book is no longer in production, Doug continues to shred his local trails and has done me the honour of writing the foreword for my new book. I'm humbled and thrilled to have him do so, and want to thank him again for playing a part in this project.

Finally, thank you to the friends who came out with me on many rides, waiting patiently on trail as I set up my camera for that perfect shot, yet again, or when I stopped to take notes of a particular section of trail we were riding. And thank you to the local bike shops and businesses that supported this project from day one. You are all behind the successful completion of this guidebook.

Happy Trails!

Picture this: flowy singletrack that goes on for miles; big alpine rides offering up some incredible 360$^0$ views of the surrounding mountains; heart pounding downhill descents with a plethora of creative Technical Trail Features to test your bike handling prowess; fun family trail rides taking you along river banks, crossing meadows and streams trickling down from the mountain tops as the snow melts. Picture all this and more for you to explore in Kananaskis Country, only a half hour drive west of Calgary.

Kananaskis Country boasts an abundant network of trails accessible by, and open to, mountain bikes. With such a vast network of backcountry trails to explore on two wheels, one could easily spend years trying to ride them all. I've personally spent the last two years riding and documenting this incredible trails network, to provide you with an informative guide on some of my favourites and maybe not-so -favourite places to ride in Kananaskis. A majority of the trails listed in this guidebook are multi-use; please ride with care and respect other trail users also out enjoying this area.

Our riding season in Kananaskis Country may be one of the shortest in western Canada, but I guarantee that it will not disappoint once the trails thaw out and become rideable. Whether it is a ride up to the famous Jumpingpound Ridge or a short spin along the Riverview Trail with your family, my hope is that this book will serve as a great tool to get more people out on their mountain bikes, exploring the vast network of incredible trails available to us. I trust it will better prepare avid riders, the young and young at heart, families and newcomers to the sport or to our area, to choose the level of ride suitable to their ability, providing countless hours of fun, exercise and adventure. I hope this book serves you well in planning your next adventure.

To help you better understand the three types of mountain biking disciplines I've described in this book, please use the following descriptions as a guide:

**All-Mountain**
All-Mountain trails are best ridden on an all-mountain bike (5"-6" travel) and include natural and manmade features, along with stunts.

**X-Country**
X-Country (Cross Country) trails are for those interested in the up as much as the down. Trails include sweet rolling singletracks that go on for miles.

**Downhill**
Downhill trails are best ridden on a BIG bike and can typically be shuttled. Trail features may include berms, wooden manmade structures referred to as Technical Trail Features (TTFs), and stunts.

If you're visiting the area for the first time or have ridden here before, please remember to respect the trails you're on; give right of way to hikers and equestrians, and remember that horses can spook at bikes so it is important to slow down and give them space. Do not ride on closed trails. Remember to carry bear spray, as you are in bear country, and always tell someone where you're heading for a ride. Cell phone reception may be bad or non-existent in certain areas, so please always plan ahead and make sure you're prepared when heading out on the trail. WATER is important; please pack lots, especially in the height of summer. I recommend bringing a windbreaker or rain jacket, just in case, and a flash light or head lamp may come in handy if you happen to venture off trail and get lost. And don't forget a snack or some form of energy. I find liquid gels and/or bars to be light and effective.

### Elk, Cougars, and Bears, Oh Me Oh My

Kananaskis Country is home to a large number of wild animals – that's what makes this such an awesome place to be. Among them are elk, cougars, and bears. Stay aware and carry bear spray at all times. It's also suggested to yell out once in a while during your ride, not to scare the crap out of other riders or to annoy your riding buddies, but so as not to spook the animals. I find this also provides a heads up to other trail users. Visit the Wildsmart website at www.wildsmart.ca or Alberta Parks website www.albertaparks.ca for more information on living with wildlife.

### How to Use this Book

I've done my best to describe the variety of mountain bike rides located in Kananaskis Country. Some of these cater to families, while others are for the seasoned rider. All trails listed have a rating system based on a bikepirate rating, a technical rating, and a physical rating. Use these ratings to help you select the most appropriate ride for your skill level.

Along with the trail ratings, I've provided you with distance, elevation, and a description of each trailhead. Use this information to plan your trip and to get to the appropriate starting point.

A quick note on elevation ratings: elevations are calculated as the total amount of elevation gained and the total amount of elevation lost (all the ups and downs) over the entire distance of an out-and-back trail or a loop. For connector trails, trails which can be combined in several ways to form a loop, such as Jumpingpound Ridge, the elevations are based on one way.

### Trail Etiquette

Last but not least, please adhere to the following rules whenever you ride. Common courtesy extended to other trail users keeps the trails we love open to riding and gives the appropriate advocacy groups more clout when requesting access to closed trails. Please keep this in mind.

- ▸ Ride on open trails only.
- ▸ Stay on the trail.
- ▸ Respect the environment and pack your garbage out.
- ▸ Stay in control of your bike.
- ▸ Respect all trail users and yield appropriately.
- ▸ Know your limitations.
- ▸ Plan ahead and let someone know where you're heading.
- ▸ Avoid riding wet and muddy trails when possible.

Enjoy the book!

## TRAIL RATINGS

The following rating system is used throughout the book to help you identify the trails right for you. I've done my best to rate all trails according to the following. All ratings in this book are provided based on my opinion only, based on the area in which you will be riding. In no way should you interpret my rating as the official rating for the trail, as this may vary. I've done the best I can to be as accurate as I can be, but you're free to form your opinion of the trails you ride and I'd be happy if you shared it with me on bikepirate.com.

bikepirate.com provides current trail condition reports, along with GPS data, photos, and videos on mountain bike trails to ride. Hundreds of trails are featured from across Canada, US and New Zealand.

### bikepirate Rating

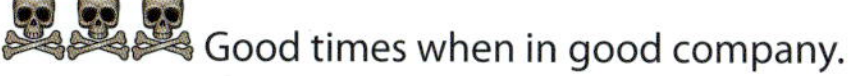 A must-do ride that I would go and do over and over again.

Highly recommend this ride; I enjoyed it heaps and would recommend it to others.

Good times when in good company.

Good trail to enjoy if you're local, but not worth a special trip.

You kidding me? No thank you, I will pass on this trail.

### Technical Ratings

**Beginner (Green):** Trails suitable for beginner and intermediate riders with gentle terrain and slope, where confidence and conditioning can be built up.

**Intermediate (Blue):** Progression to steeper grades with more difficult obstacles, offering the rider a natural progression to more advanced skills. Time to get your groove on.

**Advanced (Black):** Advanced trails will test your physical conditioning, bike handling skills, and courage. If you are unfamiliar with these trails make sure you look before you ride a feature on the route.

**Expert (Double Black):** Typically, this rating is reserved for downhill trails and bode well for circus performers and daredevils. Full armour and a high degree of skill are strongly suggested, as there is the real possibility of injury on these trails. Go forewarned.

## Physical Ratings

**Easy:** If you've never ridden, or love to eat potato chips, drink beer, and only ride once a month, this ride doesn't require any sort of fitness level and is for you.

**Moderate:** You peddle your bike a few times a week and can handle a 20 km loop without losing your cookies half way through the ride.

**Hard:** You are a fit rider that can handle a day out on the trail. In fact, you enjoy wearing spandex, shaving your legs, and pounding back Gu.

**Extreme:** You ride every day and consider pedaling up Mount Everest a warm up.

## HIDDEN TREASURES

With so many trails highlighted in this book, you might be asking yourself what rides to start to prioritize.  Depending on your skills, goals, and who you're riding with, that's a great question, with so many awesome trails to check out! I've done my best to provide you with all the information you could possibly want or need to help you select a trail or two suitable to your riding ability and style. However, thanks to a friend's recommendation, I'm also including this quick hidden treasures list for those wondering where to begin:

### Family Rides

Those looking to take their kids out for a pedal should consider the following trails/areas to ride:

- Bill Milne Bike Path
- Bow Valley Bike Path
- Nose Hill MTB Trails
- Ole Buck Loop

### Great Early Season Rides

The following rides tend to dry out early spring and can be open to riding as early as May, depending on the winter prior. Please check the bikepirate.com Trail Report or with your local trail group to make sure the trails are dry and suitable to riding. After all, riding muddy trails only destroys and erodes them.

- Prairie View to Jewell Pass Loop
- Razors Edge
- Jumpingpound Loop

### Scenic Rides

The following rides offer up some incredible scenery, along rugged backcountry trails. Most are for the advanced rider, while others may be enjoyed by the less experienced. Please read over the trail page to decide on the one suitable to your ability.

- Prairie View to Jewell Pass Loop
- Sulphur Springs Loop
- Ridgeback
- Long Distance
- Ranger Summit
- Jumpingpound Ridge to Cox Hill
- Powderface Creek to Prairie Creek Loop

**Introductory Rides**

If you're looking to get your partner, girlfriend or boyfriend, into riding, consider the following beginner to intermediate trail options.

- Family Guy
- Brakeless
- Terrace South
- Riverview Trail
- Ole Buck Loop

Free GPS Tracks: Visit bikepirate.com to download free GPS tracks for all the trails listed in this book.

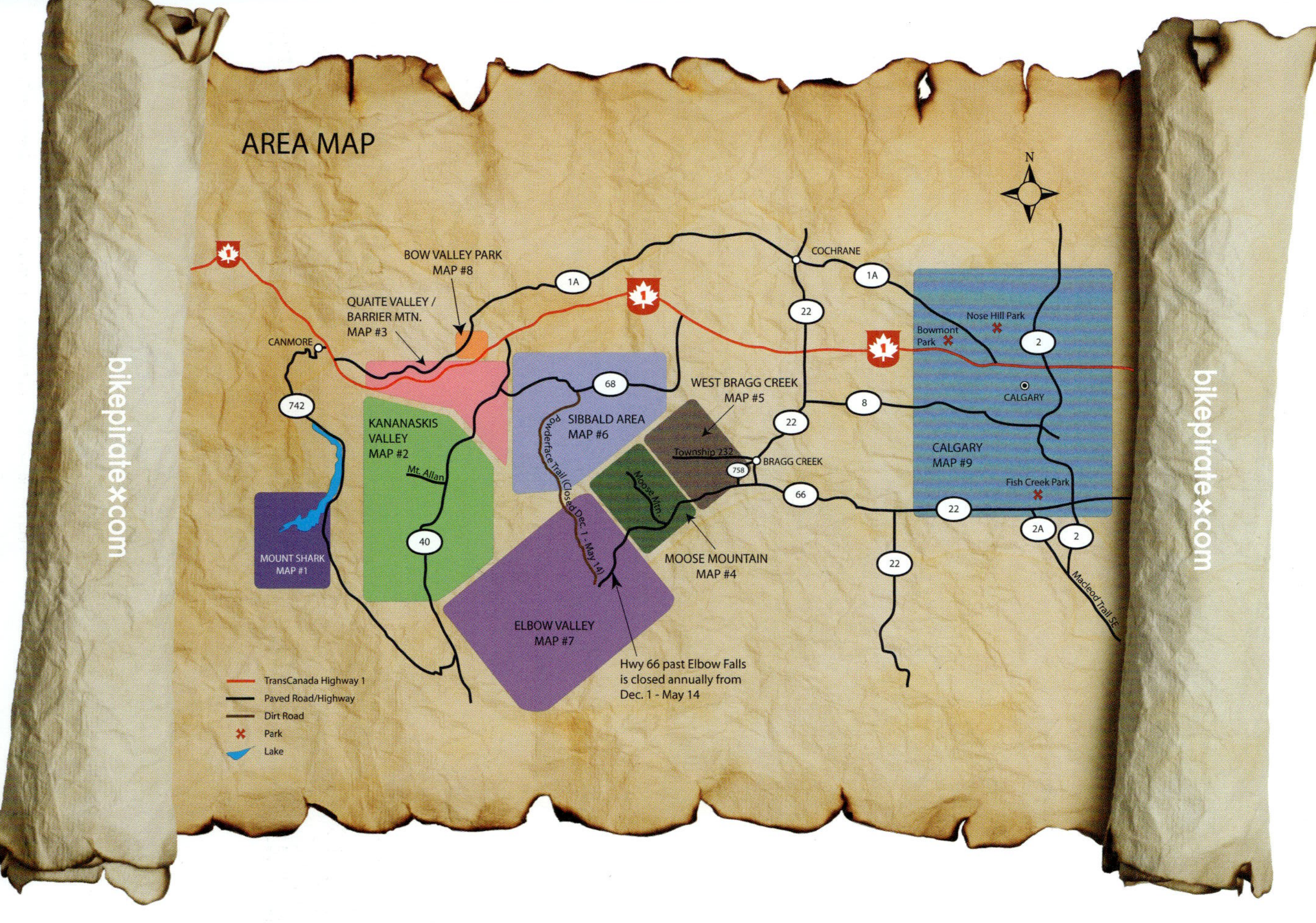

AREA MAP
N
bikepirate✖com
BOW VALLEY PARK
MAP #8
QUAITE VALLEY /
BARRIER MTN.
MAP #3
CANMORE
COCHRANE
1A
1A
22
Nose Hill Park
Bowmont Park
2
CALGARY
742
68
WEST BRAGG CREEK
MAP #5
8
KANANASKIS
VALLEY
MAP #2
SIBBALD AREA
MAP #6
Powderface Trail (Closed Dec. 1 - May 14)
22
Mt. Allan
Township 232
758
BRAGG CREEK
CALGARY
MAP #9
Moose Mtn.
66
Fish Creek Park
40
22
MOUNT SHARK
MAP #1
MOOSE MOUNTAIN
MAP #4
2A
2
22
ELBOW VALLEY
MAP #7
Hwy 66 past Elbow Falls
is closed annually from
Dec. 1 - May 14
Macleod Trail SE
TransCanada Highway 1
Paved Road/Highway
Dirt Road
Park
Lake
bikepirate✖com

lightandmotion.com
LIGHT & MOTION
» Performance and commuter lights
» USB Rechargeable
» Side lighting
» Tool-less mount
LIGHT UP YOUR RIDE

Canada's Premier High-End Mountain Bike Shop
CALGARY CYCLE
403-277-3430 | calgarycycle.com

MAP 1: MOUNT SHARK
N
Spray Lakes Reservoir
742
1800
1720
1720
1760
1920
1800
1800
1920
1720
1880
1800
1800
Mount Shark Day Use
Mount Shark Road
Watridge Lake
Watridge Lake Trail
Mount Engadine Lodge
TransCanada Highway 1
Paved Road/Highway
Dirt Road
Trailhead
Water
Height in metres (m)
1800
Beginner Trails
Intermediate Trails
Advanced / Expert Trails
Lodging
Toilets / Outhouse
Parking
300 m
SCALE
bikepirate✳com
bikepirate✳com

# 1 | MOUNT SHARK | ☠

| | |
|---|---|
| Distance: Over 20 km | Technical Rating: Beginner |
| Time: 1 - 4 hrs | Physical Rating: Moderate |
| Elevation Gain: Not applicable | Season: June - October |
| Elevation Loss: Not applicable | Trail Type: X-Country |

The Mount Shark mountain bike trails are a fun family excursion if you're looking to explore the area on two wheels. Mostly made up of grassy and gravel doubletrack, you'll be riding on x-country ski trails not maintained for summer use, aside from the Watridge Lake Trail; therefore, watch out for deadfall and expect overgrown trail.

Mount Shark offers the rider a rolling and scenic pedal on wide gravel and fire roads. Follow the well-marked 10 km loop for a roller coaster of a ride up and down the grassy doubletrack. Or head out on the well-used and maintained Watridge Lake Trail (the main trail) that takes you out towards Watridge Lake and beyond. Watridge Lake Trail is the only trail in the area which is maintained for summer use, and offers several options to stop along the trail to take in the spectacular scenery and enjoy a picnic.

Although Mount Shark is open to mountain biking, I don't recommend making a special trip out to ride this area unless you're looking to explore Mount Shark with your family and prefer to do it on your mountain bikes. You may also consider using the Watridge Lake Trail to access the area's backcountry hiking trails. Or for those adventurous types looking for a true backcountry mountain bike ride, pedal out on the Watridge Lake Trail, around Spray Lake and up the West Side Trail to connect with Goat Creek trail. At the Goat Creek junction head east along Goat Creek to Canmore or west to Banff.

### TRAILHEAD | N50 51.554 W115 22.781

From Canmore, drive 39 km south on the Smith-Dorrien / Spray Trail (Hwy 742) which begins just past the Canmore Nordic Centre. Turn right on to Mount Shark Road and continue 5 km to the Mount Shark parking lot, the main access point to all the trails in the area.

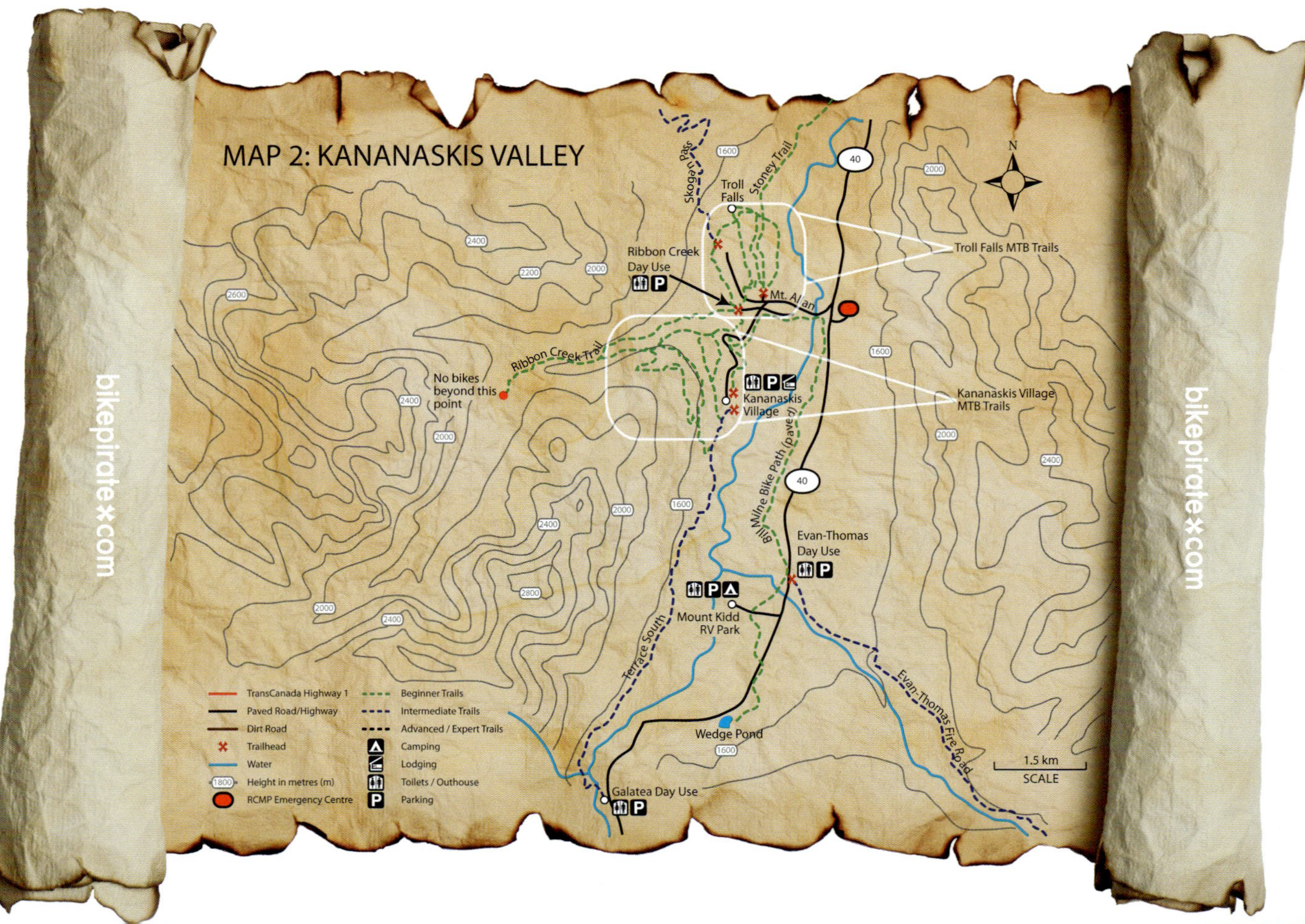
MAP 2: KANANASKIS VALLEY
N
Skogan Pass
Stoney Trail
Troll Falls
40
2000
1600
Troll Falls MTB Trails
Ribbon Creek Day Use
Mt. Allan
2400
2200
2000
2600
1600
Ribbon Creek Trail
No bikes beyond this point
2400
2000
Kananaskis Village
Kananaskis Village MTB Trails
2000
2400
Bill Milne Bike Path (paved)
40
1600
2000
Evan-Thomas Day Use
2800
2000
2400
Terrace South
Mount Kidd RV Park
Wedge Pond
1600
Evan-Thomas Fire Road
1.5 km
SCALE
Galatea Day Use
TransCanada Highway 1
Paved Road/Highway
Dirt Road
Trailhead
Water
1800  Height in metres (m)
RCMP Emergency Centre
Beginner Trails
Intermediate Trails
Advanced / Expert Trails
Camping
Lodging
Toilets / Outhouse
Parking
bikepirate✕com
bikepirate✕com

# KANANASKIS VALLEY

The Kananaskis Valley area includes the trails surrounding Kananaskis Village, located 23 km south of Hwy 1 (TransCanada), accessed via Hwy 40. One can use the Kananaskis Village as the main access to most of the mountain bike trails found in the area. Please note that all trails in the area open to mountain biking are designated multi-use, so please be respectful to other trail users when venturing out to explore this fun trails network.

A large number of the mountain bike trails located in the Kananaskis Valley are well suited to families and people with burleys. They are typically wide doubletrack trails, many of which are used for x-country skiing in the winter time. In addition, there are a handful of classic rides that stretch considerable distances, starting at or near Kananaskis Village. These longer rides are typically more demanding and better suited to intermediate and advanced riders. Trails, including Evan-Thomas Fire Road, Stoney Trail, Skogan Pass and a Whole Lotta Up, which combines the latter two trails plus many more to form an epic loop, are all found in the area. The following pages highlight all the trails open to mountain biking in Kananaskis Valley, many of which have not changed since the days they were used by hunter-gatherers and offer the rider a unique look back in time. For those looking for a short, yet fun, singletrack trail accessed via Kananaskis Village, check out the Terrace South trail. Terrace South is the only true singletrack trail located in the area.

The majority of the trails in this area are accessed via Ribbon Creek Day Use Area or via Kananaskis Village.  Plenty of parking and access to toilets are offered at all of these locations. Evan-Thomas Fire Road is accessed via Evan-Thomas Day Use Area, about 5 km south of the Village.

## 2 | BILL MILNE BIKE PATH | ☠ ☠ ☠

| | |
|---|---|
| Distance: 11 km (one way) | Technical Rating: Beginner |
| Time: 1 - 2 hrs | Physical Rating: Easy |
| Elevation Gain: 116 m | Season: May - October |
| Elevation Loss: 122 m | Trail Type: Paved pathway |

The Bill Milne Bike Path (formerly named Evan-Thomas) is a fully paved path connecting Kananaskis Village to the Wedge Pond Day Use area. This path is great for families, the young and the young at heart. Similar to the Banff Legacy Trail, but further set back from the highway (Hwy 40), the Bill Milne is a nice and easy pedal for all to enjoy.

The fully-paved path gently winds and rolls along the Evan-Thomas Creek, crossing it in several places. Since there is no major elevation gain on this ride, just sit back and enjoy the mountain views, the diverse vegetation, and the soothing creek running mostly parallel to the path. Bill Milne may be ridden as an out-and-back or taken as one-way trail if you've arranged to have someone pick you up at the Wedge Pond carpark. It is a multi-use path, so watch out for dog walkers, hikers and kids on trikes. About 8.5 km down the trail from the Delta Hotel, there is a great place to stop for a snack, a refreshing beverage or a delicious ice cream, if you're in need of a pick me up. It's the Mount Kidd RV Park, located on the west side of the pathway; it's on the right side of the path if you're riding south. Also, consider bringing your swim trunks to take a dip in Wedge Pond to cool off on a hot day, before beginning your pedal back to Kananaskis Village.

This is not a singletrack ride or a ripping trail, but rather a nice and mellow path for when you need a break from riding hard or a great ride if you're looking to spend some time with the family on two wheels.

### TRAILHEAD | N50 55.242 W115 08.882

Take Hwy 1 (TransCanada) to Hwy 40 south towards Kananaskis Village. Exit Hwy 40 at Kananaskis Village turn-off and park near the Delta Lodge. From the Village/Delta, pedal north on Centennial Drive for a few hundred metres before turning east (right) onto the Bill Milne Bike Path; it is clearly marked. Hint: you will drive by the trailhead located to your right on your way to the Village parking.

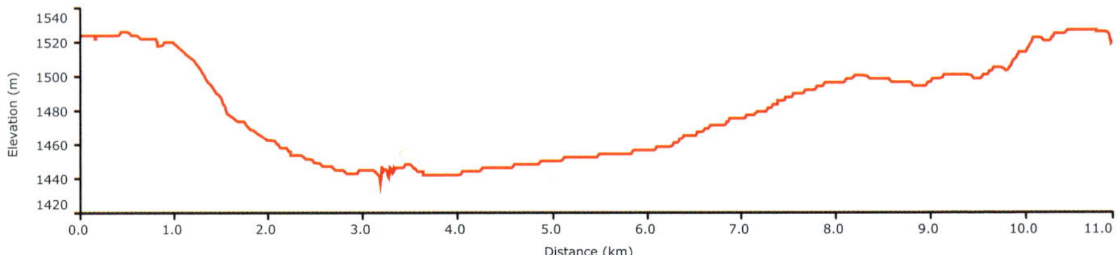

# 3 | KANANASKIS VILLAGE MTB TRAILS | 💀💀

| | |
|---|---|
| Distance: Over 15 km | Technical Rating: Beginner - Intermediate |
| Time: 1 - 3 hrs | Physical Rating: Easy - Moderate |
| Elevation Gain: Not applicable | Season: June - October |
| Elevation Loss: Not applicable | Trail Type: X-Country |

Kananaskis Village Mountain Bike Trails are well suited to recreational mountain bikers and their families. The wide open doubletrack trails consisting of grass and dirt make for an easy afternoon pedal. During the summer months you may find that the Aspen Trail gets a little overgrown. Instead, take the Kovach trail out from the Village and come back along Terrace Trail to form a fun, yet scenic, loop to do with your family.

The small networks of trails are good for cruising on, wide enough for your burley and a great way to access the Troll Falls MTB Trails or the Ribbon Creek Trail right from Kananaskis Village. A majority of the short trails pop in and out of the trees, exposing you to some incredible views of the surrounding mountains.

## TRAILHEAD | N50 55.015 W115 08.749 (OUTFITTERS)

Access the trails right from Kananaskis Village. Start with Terrace or Kovach located near the parking lot by the ball diamond in the Village. Or head over to Kananaskis Outfitters and from there you will find arrows/directions pointing you to the various trailheads.

# 4 | RIBBON CREEK | ☠ ☠

| | |
|---|---|
| Distance: 8.5 km (return) | Technical Rating: Beginner |
| Time: 1 - 2 hrs | Physical Rating: Easy |
| Elevation Gain: 144 m | Season: May - October |
| Elevation Loss: 144 m | Trail Type: X-Country |

Ribbon Creek trail is an out-and-back beginner ride, which may be combined with the Kovach trail to form a loop around Ribbon Creek. The trail may be accessed via the Ribbon Creek Day Use Area, the same spot as the Troll Falls MTB Trails.

A short 4.25 km pedal up a gentle slope on a wide gravel path is what one can expect from this scenic ride. It's a great ride for families looking to explore the Kananaskis Village area trails without getting in over their heads. The trail runs along the river valley with Olympic Peak (Nakiska Ski Resort) and Ribbon Peak to your right and Mount Kidd appearing in the distance to your left.

The Ribbon Creek trail continues past the 4.25 km mark, where bikes are not allowed, as clearly indicated by the "no bikes" sign. Turn around at this point, or continue on foot for another 4.2 km to reach Ribbon Falls. A bike rack is available, so bring a lock if you decide to venture on.

## TRAILHEAD | N50 55.990 W115 08.855 (RIBBON CREEK TH)

The trailhead for Ribbon Creek is located at the Ribbon Creek Day Use Area. If driving, take Hwy 40 to the Kananaskis Village turn-off (Mount Allan Drive). Drive a few hundred metres on Mount Allan and turn left onto Centennial Drive, followed by a quick right to the well-marked Ribbon Creek Day Use Area.

If staying at the Kananaskis Village, take Terrace Proper/North or the Bill Milne Bike Path to access the trail located 1.5 km north of the Village.

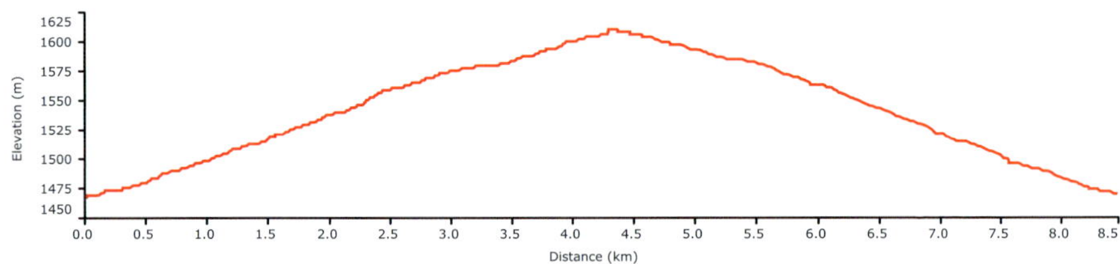

# 5 | STONEY TRAIL | 💀 💀

| | |
|---|---|
| Distance: 20 km (one way; north) | Technical Rating: Beginner |
| Time: 2 - 4 hrs | Physical Rating: Easy |
| Elevation Gain: 290 m | Season: *April - October |
| Elevation Loss: 408 m | Trail Type: X-Country |

Stoney Trail is mostly an easy rolling doubletrack that may be ridden either direction, one way, or used as a connector to Barrier Lake Day Use area, the Bow Valley Park interchange, or the Ribbon Creek Day Use Area, depending on which way you ride this trail. We recommend riding Stoney from the Stoney carpark if you're out for a family outing, as the elevation gained is less and you can access it directly from Kananaskis Village using a network of trails and pathways.

This trail is not for the hardcore mountain biker, but rather well suited to a family outing. One can expect a nice scenic ride that follows the power lines along beautiful grassy meadows and mixed forests. The smoothest section of trail lies between Ribbon Creek and the Jewell Pass junction. North of Jewell the trail does get considerably narrower in a number of sections (singletrack), with added roots and loose rock, before opening up again on some nice and wide doubletrack once you near the Bow Valley Park interchange.

*Please note there is an annual closure in effect from April 15 – June 15 on the section of trail heading south from Jewell Pass to Troll Falls.

## TRAILHEAD | N50 56.189 W115 08.475 (STONEY CARPARK)

The trailhead, when riding the trail north from Kananaskis Village (recommended), is located at the Stoney Trail parking area. Exit on to Mount Allan Drive from Hwy 40 and take your first right into the Stoney carpark, just past Centennial Drive seen to your left.

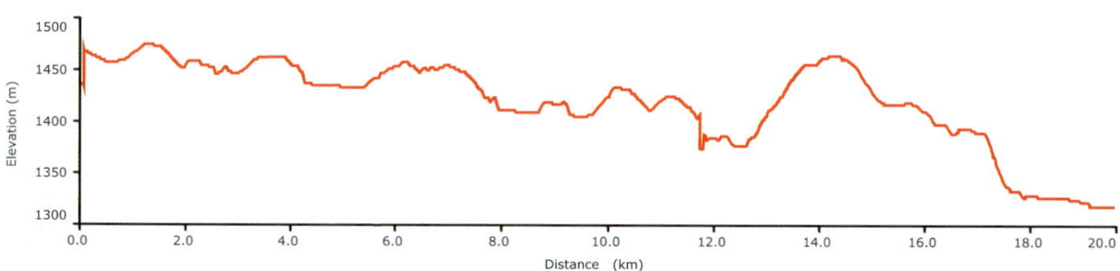

# 6 | TROLL FALLS MTB TRAILS | 💀 💀 💀

| | |
|---|---|
| Distance: Under 10 km | Technical Rating: Beginner |
| Time: 1 - 3 hrs | Physical Rating: Easy - Moderate |
| Elevation Gain: Not applicable | Season: May - October |
| Elevation Loss: Not applicable | Trail Type: X-Country |

The trails of Troll Falls are well suited to recreational mountain bikers and their families. Unless you're heading out on Skogan Pass, an epic ride, the wide open doubletrack trails consisting of grass and dirt make for an easy afternoon pedal.

The small network of trails are good for cruising on, wide enough for your burley and a great way to access Troll Falls – a "must visit" if you're new to the area. To access the falls, please lock your bike up or hide it in the woods, before heading up the last 300 m of trail. This section of trail has eroded over the years, is tough to ride, and is much easier when walked. It's encouraged that everyone walk this stretch as not to erode the trail any further.

Accessed via the Ribbon Creek parking lot, or directly from the Kananaskis Village, or via the Stoney parking lot (the more popular start point), the Troll Falls trail network offers some breathtaking scenery. To the west is the Nakiska Ski Area, to the east is the Kananaskis River and to the north are Troll Falls. A majority of the short trails pop in and out of the trees, exposing you to some incredible views, while making their way to the main junction at Troll Falls. From there you can double back or choose a different trail to return on.

## TRAILHEAD | N50 55.990 W115 08.855 (RIBBON CREEK TH)

The trailhead for the Troll Falls MTB Trails is located at the Ribbon Creek Day Use Area and parking lot. If driving, take Hwy 40 to the Kananaskis Village turn-off (Mount Allan Drive). Drive a few hundred metres and turn left onto Centennial Drive, followed by a quick right to Ribbon Creek Day Use Area, which is clearly marked. From there reference the map and create your own adventure.

If staying at the Kananaskis Village, take Terrace Proper/North or the Bill Milne Bike Path to access these trails located 1.5 km north of the Village.

To access the trails via Stoney Trail carpark, exit Hwy 40 onto Mount Allan Road and take your first right off Mount Allan into the Stoney carpark. It is well marked.

# 7 | EVAN-THOMAS FIRE ROAD | 💀 💀

**Distance:** 30 km (return)  
**Time:** 4 - 6 hrs  
**Elevation Gain:** 928 m  
**Elevation Loss:** 928 m

**Technical Rating:** Intermediate  
**Physical Rating:** Hard  
**Season:** July - October  
**Trail Type:** X-Country

Evan-Thomas is an old exploration road which gradually ascends to Evan-Thomas Pass. Frequented by local outfitters, the trail has seen better days. After the 1.5 km mark the trail is not maintained and can be loose, wet and boggy in sections, making for an interesting pedal up.

As this is an out-an-back, unless you plan on continuing on to the Elbow River, you may choose to turn around at the 9 km mark, after which the trail condition deteriorates further, making it a challenging ride on the last 6 km to the pass. To Elbow River, the trail is approximately another 7 km from the pass to where it joins Elbow Trail. From Elbow Trail continue on for another 12 km to the Little Elbow Campground for a total of 34 km (one way).

Evan-Thomas runs on mostly wide doubletrack surrounded by trees, offering up a number of viewpoints when you pop out of the woods. The trees will thin in a few sections, just enough to provide glimpses of Evan-Thomas Creek running parallel to the trail. There are a number of creek crossings, which are sure to get your feet wet. This is especially the case in the spring, when the water levels are running high, possibly making the creek crossings impassable. Avoid riding this trail after it has rained due to the high equestrian use.

## TRAILHEAD | N50 53.609 W115 08.034

Take Hwy 1 to Hwy 40 south. Drive about 27 km south on Hwy 40 to the Evan-Thomas Day Use Area, which is off Hwy 40 and well-marked. The trailhead starts right from the parking lot.

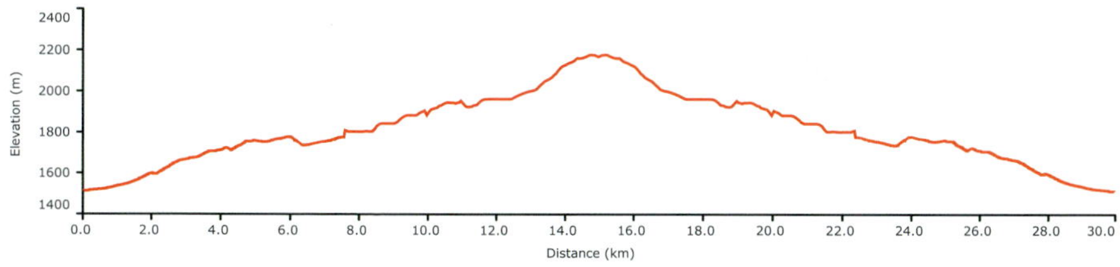

# 8 | SKOGAN PASS | 💀 💀 💀 💀

**Distance:** 18.8 km (one way)
**Time:** 2 - 3 hrs
**Elevation Gain:** 742 m
**Elevation Loss:** 766 m

**Technical Rating:** Intermediate
**Physical Rating:** Hard
**Season:** June - October
**Trail Type:** X-Country

Skogan Pass is one of the longer and more epic rides in Kananaskis Valley, connecting the Ribbon Creek Day Use Area (near Kananaskis Village) with the Bow Valley near Canmore. It is best ridden from Ribbon Creek if you're looking for more flow and a gentler climb up to the Pass. The descent down to Pigeon Creek is fast and fun, but watch out for hikers or riders coming the opposite direction and bears.

Skogan Pass is a Norwegian word meaning a magic forest with elves and trolls. Ride it as a part of the big epic ride, Whole Lotta Up, and you might just be seeing elves and trolls near the end of your ride.

From Ribbon Creek follow the well-marked trail made up of dirt and gravel which gradually climbs the doubletrack all the way to Skogan Pass. A short side trip (400 m return) to Skogan Pass Viewpoint is highly recommended and found about 10 km up the trail. Once you hit Skogan Pass, the fast and loose descent begins all the way to the Banff Gate Mountain Resort parking area, the end of the trail. If you didn't organize a shuttle, you can turn around and ride the trail in reverse or continue on to Jewell Pass and return via Stoney Trail; see the description for Whole Lotta Up.

**TRAILHEAD | N50 55.965 W115 08.864 (RIBBON CREEK); N51 01.590 W115 14.584 (RESORT)**

South access: Take Hwy 40 south to the Kananaskis Village turn-off (Mount Allan Drive). Drive a few hundred metres on Mount Allan and turn left onto Centennial Drive, followed by a quick right to the Ribbon Creek Day Use Area. Signs point in the direction of the trailhead for Skogan Pass.

North access: Take Hwy 1 to the Dead Man's Flats interchange. Exit and drive south to the parking lot near Banff Gate Mountain Resort. The trailhead is accessed from the parking lot.

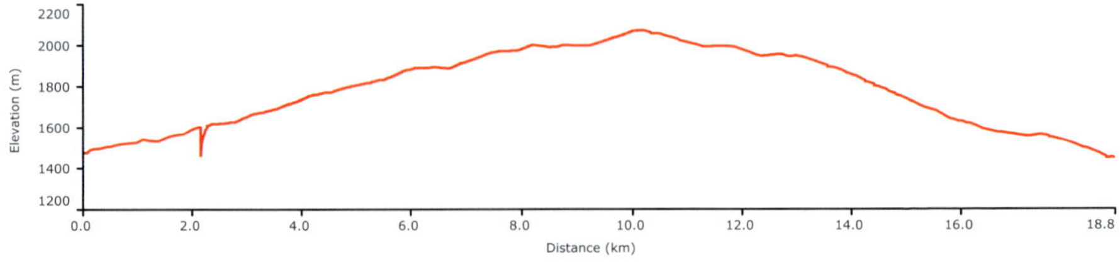



*Find the Hidden Treasures: A Guide to Mountain Bike Trails in Kananaskis Country*

# 9 | TERRACE SOUTH | 💀 💀 💀

**Distance:** 15.6 km (return)
**Time:** 1.5 – 2.5 hrs
**Elevation Gain:** 287 m
**Elevation Loss:** 290 m

**Technical Rating:** Intermediate
**Physical Rating:** Moderate
**Season:** May - October
**Trail Type:** X-Country

Terrace South is a singletrack trail with minimal elevation gains that runs high above the Kananaskis River and Golf Course. It is the only true singletrack trail found right at Kananaskis Village's doorstep and a great ride to explore. Mainly ridden as an out-and-back, the trail may also be ridden one-way, from either the Village or from the opposite end starting at the Galatea Day Use Area, or as a loop. To ride Terrace South as a loop, combine it with the paved Bill Milne Bike Path, creating a ride just under 20 km.

There are a number of great viewpoints along this trail that overlook the golf course and river below. A short creek bed crossing is thrown in for good measure, which may keep things interesting during the spring months when the creek runs high and may be found impassible. The crossing is found at about the 5.7 km mark down the trail.

The Terrace South singletrack is mostly buff, flowy, and fast, with a few rooty and rocky bits found south of the creek bed crossing. The last part of trail crosses over the Kananaskis River on a wooden suspension bridge, well worth checking out. Following the bridge is a short pedal up a steep hill which provides access to the Galatea Day Use Area and parking.

**TRAILHEAD | N50 55.096 W115 08.892 (VILLAGE RIM); N50 54.947 W115 09.024 (TH)**

Start at the Kananaskis Outfitters (Kananaskis Village) and ride west up the well-marked Village Rim Trail to the Terrace South Trailhead, about 380 m from the Kananaskis Outfitters. The trailhead is well signed.

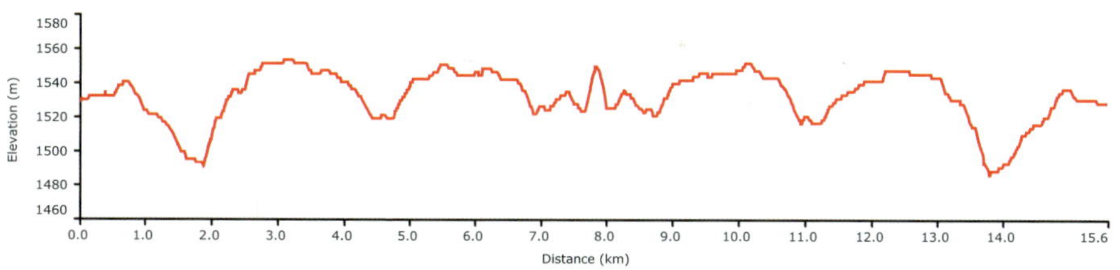

MAP 2.1: WHOLE LOTTA UP
Dead Man's Flats
Bow Corridor Link Trail
George Biggy St.
Heart Creek Day Use
Quaite Valley Connector
Quaite Valley
Heart Mountain
Jewell Pass
Barrier Lake
Mount Baldy
Pigeon Mountain
Banff Gate Mountain Resort
Mount Lorette
Skogan Pass Viewpoint
Skogan Pass
Stoney Trail
Ribbon Creek Day Use
Mt. Allan
N
TransCanada Highway 1
Paved Road/Highway
Dirt Road
Trailhead
Water
Height in metres (m)
Beginner Trails
Intermediate Trails
Advanced / Expert Trails
Lodging
Toilets / Outhouse
Parking
1.5 km
SCALE
Start at Ribbon Creek Day Use taking Skogan Pass trail; follow the signs to the trailhead from the parking area. Skogan finishes at Pigeon Creek parking lot. From there ride the dirt road north towards Hwy 1 and look for the Bow Corridor Link Trail. Take the Bow Corridor Link Trail east (right-side of road). Once you hit the Heart Creek day use area, continue along Quaite Valley Connector east to Quaite Valley. Climb south (right) up Quaite Valley. At the Prairie View and Jewell Pass Junction, take Jewell Pass southeast all the way to Stoney Trail. Turn right (south) on to Stoney Trail and complete the loop by returning to the Ribbon Creek Day Use area.

# 10 | WHOLE LOTTA UP | 💀 💀 💀 💀

| | |
|---|---|
| Distance: 52 km | Technical Rating: Advanced |
| Time: 5 - 7 hrs | Physical Rating: Extreme |
| Elevation Gain: 1,600 m | Season: June 15 - October |
| Elevation Loss: 1,609 m | Trail Type: X-Country |

Whole Lotta Up is an epic x-country ride that begins at the Ribbon Creek Day Use Area and parking lot in Kananaskis Village. The trail combines a number of "must do" rides to form a large loop circling Pigeon Mountain, Mount McGillivray, Heart Mountain and Mary Barclay's Mountain back to the Ribbon Creek parking lot.

To start this epic adventure, park at Ribbon Creek and pedal up Skogan Pass; follow the signs to the trailhead from the parking area. Skogan Pass trail is the first leg of your journey and is best ridden northwest, making the climbing bearable as the trail gradually takes you up to the Pass. The views from the Skogan Pass Viewpoint are fantastic and well worth the short 200 m side trip to access the lookout. From the lookout, return to the main trail and continue north up Skogan Pass Trail; the Pass is not far off. A fast and wide singletrack descent down to Pigeon Creek begins once you've hit the Pass. At the bottom of the descent, from the parking lot, ride the dirt road towards Hwy 1 and look for the Bow Corridor Link Trail to your right. Jump on the Bow Corridor Link to head east. This is an advanced to expert trail which will challenge the most competent rider, especially after completing the first leg of this journey. Once you hit the Heart Creek Day Use Area, continue on Quaite Valley Connector east to Quaite Valley. This is a short, fun, and fast singletrack trail that will give your legs a break before hitting the long and steep Quaite Valley climb. Ride up (south) Quaite Valley to the Prairie View and Jewell Pass Junction, taking Jewell Pass southeast all the way to Stoney Trail. Once on Stoney, the home stretch, continue south (right) back to the Ribbon Creek parking lot. The last stretch is wide open and can be really hot in the sun, so make sure to pack loads of water and refreshments for this ride.

## TRAILHEAD | N50 55.970 W115 08.874

Take Hwy 40 south to the Kananaskis Village turn-off (Mount Allan Drive). Drive a few hundred metres on Mount Allan and turn left onto Centennial Drive, followed by a quick right to Ribbon Creek Day Use Area. From there the ride starts up Skogan Pass Trail, which is well marked.

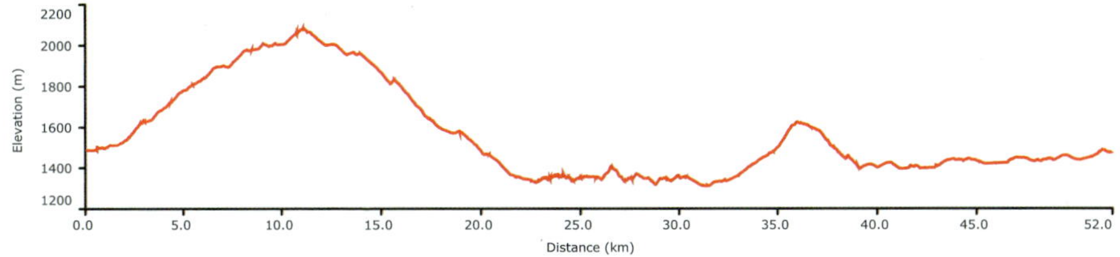

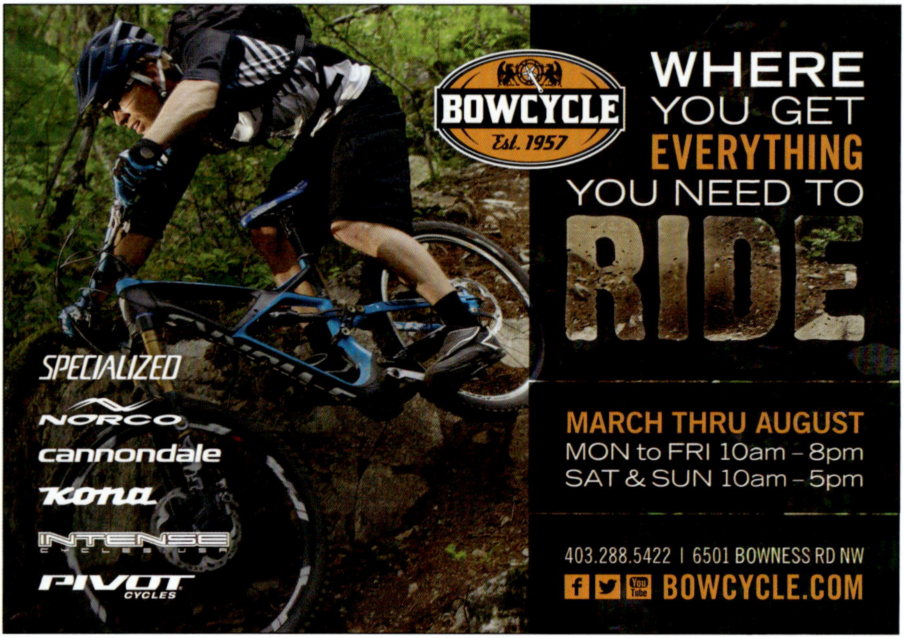
BOWCYCLE
Est. 1957
WHERE YOU GET EVERYTHING YOU NEED TO
RIDE
SPECIALIZED
NORCO
cannondale
Kona
INTENSE CYCLES USA
PIVOT CYCLES
MARCH THRU AUGUST
MON to FRI 10am – 8pm
SAT & SUN 10am – 5pm
403.288.5422 | 6501 BOWNESS RD NW
BOWCYCLE.COM

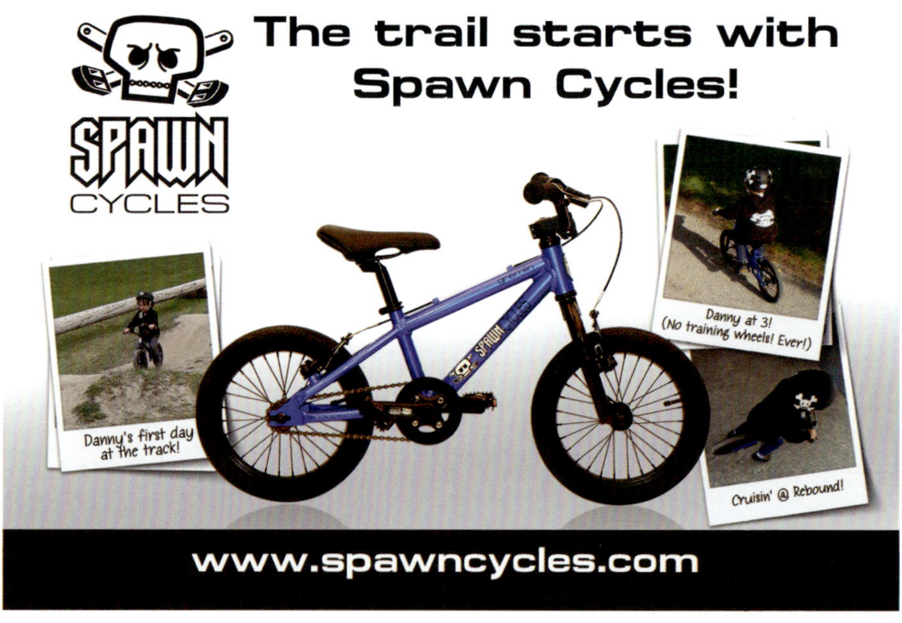
SPAWN CYCLES
The trail starts with Spawn Cycles!
Danny's first day at the track!
Danny at 3! (No training wheels! Ever!)
Cruisin' @ Rebound!
www.spawncycles.com

MAP 3: QUAITE VALLEY / BARRIER MTN.
N
1A
1A
Exshaw
Lac des Arcs
Bow Corridor Link Trail
Quaite Valley Connector
Quaite Valley
1600
Razors Edge
Prairie View
Stoney Trail
Stoney Trail
40
Bow Valley Park Interchange
1600
Barrier Dam Day Use
Dead Man's Flats
1400
1600
Heart Creek Day Use
Heart Mountain
1800
2000
1600
Jewell Pass
1800
1400
Barrier Lake
68
Banff Gate Mountain Resort
Pigeon Mountain
1600
1800
Mount McGillivray
U of C Field Station
Skogan Pass
2000
2000
Mount Baldy
Lusk Pass
1600
1800
2000
2400
1400
Stoney Trail
Mount Lorette
2000
Baldy Pass
40
1800
1600
2000
1800
Skogan Pass
1600
1600
2000
1.5 km
SCALE
TransCanada Highway 1
Paved Road/Highway
Dirt Road
Trailhead
Water
1800    Height in metres (m)
Beginner Trails
Intermediate Trails
Advanced / Expert Trails
Lodging
Toilets / Outhouse
Parking
bikepirate✕com
bikepirate✕com

# QUAITE VALLEY / BARRIER MOUNTAIN

Quaite Valley/Barrier Mountain falls into the Kananaskis Valley area, but has been separated out in this book because of the short distance from the Town of Canmore and the two distinct access points. Access to the trails may be gained via Heart Creek Day Use Area or via Barrier Dam Day Use Area. Heart Creek is 16 km east of Canmore and serves those riders coming from the west. Riders coming from the east may find that Barrier Dam Day Use Area, about 9 km south of Hwy 1, on Hwy 40, provides better access. Where you choose to park will depend on the trails you are out to ride. Please reference the map on the previous page to help with your decision.

The trails found in Quaite Valley/Barrier Mountain include a variety of singletrack and doubletrack trails ranging from the classic ride, Prairie View to Jewell Pass, to the newly built all-mountain trail, Razors Edge. You won't be disappointed with the riding found in this area, most of which can be ridden within 2 – 4 hours depending on the loop/trail you take.

# 11 | QUAITE VALLEY | 💀 💀

| | |
|---|---|
| Distance: 4.1 km | Technical Rating: Intermediate |
| Time: 25 min - 1 hr | Physical Rating: Hard |
| Elevation Gain: 301 m | Season: June - October |
| Elevation Loss: 4 m | Trail Type: X-Country |

Quaite Valley trail is an important connector trail, linking to the Jewell Pass, Prairie View and Razors Edge trails. The trail on its own is not one that makes me jump with joy, but when used to connect to one of the three trails mentioned, or looped embracing all three, one can easily see why Quaite Valley is an integral part of the Quaite Valley/ Barrier Mountain area trails network. Connect to Quaite Valley by parking in the Heart Creek Day Use Area, riding the Quaite Valley Connector west to the Quaite Valley trail. Alternatively, the trail may be accessed via Prairie View or Jewell Pass.

Quaite Valley is all doubletrack which starts off easy enough up a wide gravel path. Once you reach the Quaite Valley Backcountry Campground, Quaite Valley becomes much more demanding as the grade steepens and the gravel path turns to roots, rocks and boulders. Climbing up this trail is not a lot of fun, but coming down is fantastical. The trail ends at the junction to Prairie View and Jewell Pass. If you were to continue on up Prairie View for about 500 m, you would access the trailhead for Razors Edge.

## TRAILHEAD | N51 03.754 W115 07.984 (TH); N51 03.600 W115 07.954 (CONNECTOR)

Access the trailhead via Quaite Valley Connector. Park at the Heart Creek Day Use Area, located off Hwy 1, east of Dead Man's Flats. Ride west on Quaite Valley Connector until you reach the clearly marked Quaite Valley Trail. From there turn right (south) to begin climbing Quaite Valley.

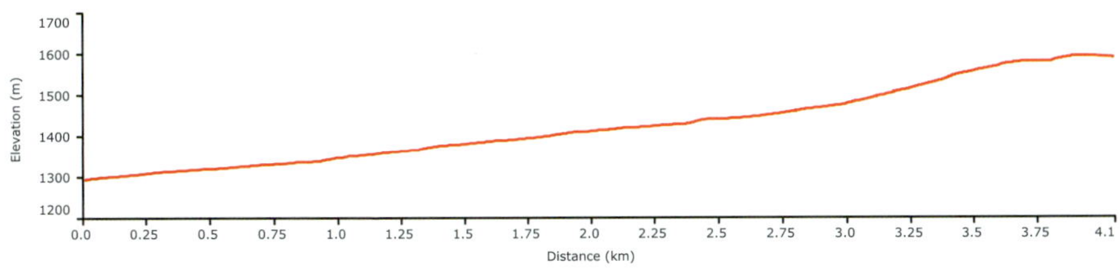

# 12 | QUAITE VALLEY CONNECTOR | ☠☠☠

| | |
|---|---|
| Distance: 2.9 km | Technical Rating: Intermediate |
| Time: 15 - 45 min | Physical Rating: Moderate |
| Elevation Gain: 62 m | Season: June - October |
| Elevation Loss: 61 m | Trail Type: X-Country |

Quaite Valley Connector is a fun intermediate singletrack trail which connects Heart Creek Day Use Area with the Quaite Valley trail. Also referred to as the Quaite Creek Trail, the Quaite Connector is a short and fast trail, with a few roots and rocks thrown in for good measure. No real ups or downs are found on this trail as it follows the contour line across to Quaite Valley.

Ride this trail as a quick out-and-back, or to connect with Quaite Valley. One can also use this as an extension to the Bow Corridor Link Trail, running from Dead Man's Flats, to create a superb x-country/all-mountain singletrack ride out-and-back. When riding out on the trail from Heart Creek keep left at the main junctions and left over the bridge. If you start descending down to the highway, you may have taken a few too many lefts. Backtrack and continue eastward along the trail.

### TRAILHEAD | N51 02.848 W115 09.845

The Quaite Valley Connector trailhead is accessed via the Heart Creek Day Use Area, just east of Dead Man's Flats. Park at Heart Creek and access the trail at the end of the parking lot, located next to the large Heart Creek sign.

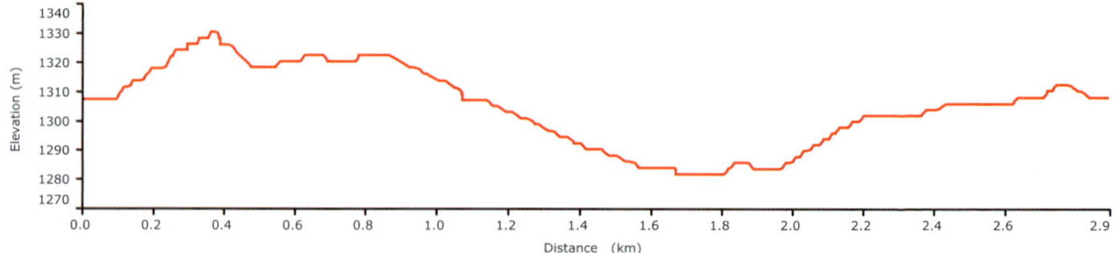

# 13 | BALDY PASS | 💀 💀 💀 💀

| | |
|---|---|
| Distance: 20.2 km | Technical Rating: Advanced |
| Time: 2 – 4 hrs | Physical Rating: Hard |
| Elevation Gain: 604 m | Season: June - October |
| Elevation Loss: 604 m | Trail Type: X-Country |

The Baldy Pass loop combines graded old roads with a bit of singletrack that climbs up into the basin back of Baldy Mountain. The climb is gentle for the first 6 km, after which point it gets narrow and steep as you approach the final few switchbacks. The views from the basin are amazing on a clear day and give you a chance to catch your breath while you take them in and prepare for the descent.

The steep, technical, and loose singletrack descent down to the valley below is super fun. Expect off-camber tight singletrack with lots of roots and rocks. If you're not up for the ride down, which starts off with 300 m of loose scree, then consider turning around and heading back the way you came. Wet weather makes the ride down that much harder and definitely ups the technical rating.

Near the end of the Baldy Pass descent, the trail will split. Stay right at the junction and continue down the remainder of the fun, fast, and super technical descent leading out on to Hwy 40 at the valley bottom. A short 5.6 km ride north (right) along the highway will take you back to the parking lot and trailhead.

## TRAILHEAD | N51 01.700 W115 02.023 (PARKING), N51 01.760 W115 01.852 (TH)

Parking is located at the Colonel's Cabin parking lot at the University of Calgary Field Station on Hwy 40, 9 km south of Hwy 1. From there follow the gravel road to your left (northwest) - you'll pass a number of cabins as you head to the start of Baldy Pass, about 300 m from the parking lot. There will be a closed gate with a TransCanada Trail sign indicating the start of Baldy.

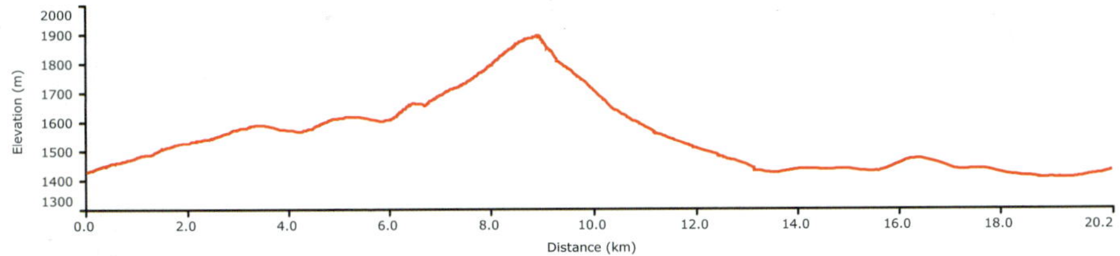

# 14 | JEWELL PASS | 💀 💀 💀 💀

| | |
|---|---|
| Distance: 2.8 km | Technical Rating: Advanced |
| Time: 15 – 45 min | Physical Rating: Moderate |
| Elevation Gain: 13 m | Season: June - October |
| Elevation Loss: 219 m | Trail Type: X-Country |

Jewell Pass is a classic singletrack trail located in the Quaite Valley/ Barrier Mountain Area near Dead Man's Flats. Typically ridden as a part of the Prairie View to Jewell Pass Loop or the Whole Lotta Up Loop, Jewell Pass may also be ridden as an out-and-back accessed via Stoney Trail from Barrier Dam. The trail offers scenic views of the spectacular Barrier Lake and provides access to the secluded Jewell Falls, which are definitely worth checking out. When ridden as a part of the Prairie View Loop, the trail is a fast and exciting descent down to Stoney Trail. Aside from a short, steep climb near the end of the trail, this technical singletrack, made up of roots and rocks, rapidly descends the mountainside to Jewell Creek where it crosses the creek several times. After the first creek crossing the trail gets a little more challenging, with several sections that include large boulders to navigate over or around. For advanced riders this section will prove to be a fun and fast obstacle course, where several boulders may be used as short launching pads to keep you moving forward. Intermediate riders will find this section challenging, but good practice to advance their skills.

Please watch out for other trails users when riding Jewell Pass, as this is a multi-use trail that may be ridden in either direction. My suggestion is to ride Jewell Pass north to south for maximum flow.

## TRAILHEAD | N51 01.499 W115 04.818 (SOUTH TH); N51 02.651 W115 05.759 (NORTH TH)

Jewell Pass may be accessed via Stoney Trail, Quaite Valley or Prairie View. To access the trail via Stoney, park at the Barrier Dam picnic area located just off of Hwy 40, 8 km south of Hwy 1. From the parking area pedal across Barrier Dam and follow Stoney Trail south to the turn-off for Jewell Pass, which is  clearly marked.

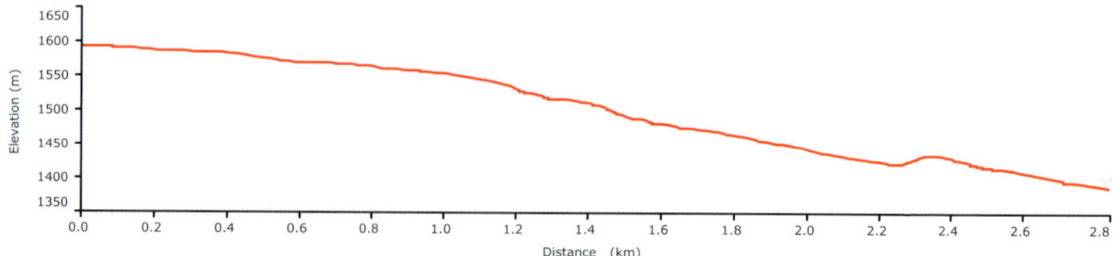

# 15 | PRAIRIE VIEW TO JEWELL PASS LOOP | 

| | |
|---|---|
| Distance: 15 km | Technical Rating: Advanced |
| Time: 2 - 4 hrs | Physical Rating: Hard |
| Elevation Gain: 649 m | Season: June - October |
| Elevation Loss: 647 m | Trail Type: X-Country |

This super fun and scenic ride takes you up Barrier Mountain to a sweet panoramic view of the surrounding mountains, prairies, and rivers. A popular trail among mountain bikers and hikers alike, expect it to be busy on weekends and evenings in the summer months.

A 6 km gravel road climb with a large number of switchbacks takes you up Barrier Mountain to a short hike-a-bike section near the top. The climb to the top is very tough and relentless, but is rewarded with a super-fast and technical descent down to Jewel Pass summit. From there you will head left (south) onto Jewel Pass; the ride is a challenging singletrack, looping you back to the parking lot. Keep left on all major junctions to get back to the start of the Barrier Mountain climb; from there head right (east) back to Barrier Dam parking.

## TRAILHEAD | N51 01.933 W115 02.353

The trailhead starts at the Barrier Dam picnic and parking area located off Hwy 40, 8 km south of Hwy 1. Follow the gravel road, crossing the power lines, up to the fork in the trail. Look for a map indicating the start of the Prairie View climb 2 km from the parking lot.

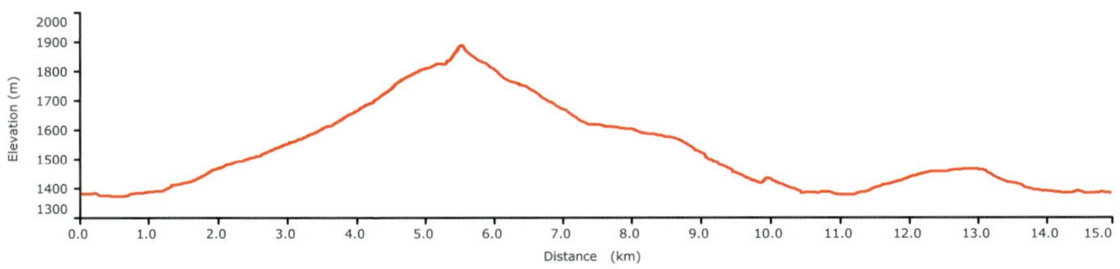

# 16 | BOW CORRIDOR LINK TRAIL | ☠ ☠ ☠

| | |
|---|---|
| Distance: 7.6 km (one way) | Technical Rating: Expert |
| Time: 1 - 2 hrs | Physical Rating: Moderate |
| Elevation Gain: 226 m | Season: May - October |
| Elevation Loss: 229 m | Trail Type: All-Mountain |

The Bow Corridor Link Trail is a part of the TransCanada trail network and links the hamlet of Deadman's Flats to the popular Heart Creek Day Use area. This particular section of trail runs almost 8 km and is rated expert for a good portion of trail. A challenging singletrack with Technical Trail Features (TTFs) including stairs, ladders and bridges, makes this an exciting ride for the experienced rider. Expect short, but steep, uphills and narrow singletrack that runs along the edge of a ravine for portions of the trail.

Bow Corridor Link Trail is around 80% singletrack with a short section of four-wheel drive trail. It may be looped as a part of a larger, more intense ride combining Skogan Pass, Quaite Valley, Jewell Pass and Stoney referred to as Whole Lotta Up. Or ride it one way or as an out-and-back. The preferred way to ride this trail is out towards Heart Creek as it tends to flow better and going down the stairs is much easier than going up.

## TRAILHEAD | N51 02.244 W115 15.290 (DEAD MAN'S)

To access the trail from Dead Man's Flats take Hwy 1 to Dead Man's Flat exit (George Biggy Sr. Road). The trailhead is located on the south side of Hwy 1 on George Biggy Sr. Road. Look for the entrance about 200 m in the trees on the east side of George Biggy Sr. Road; it is very well signed.

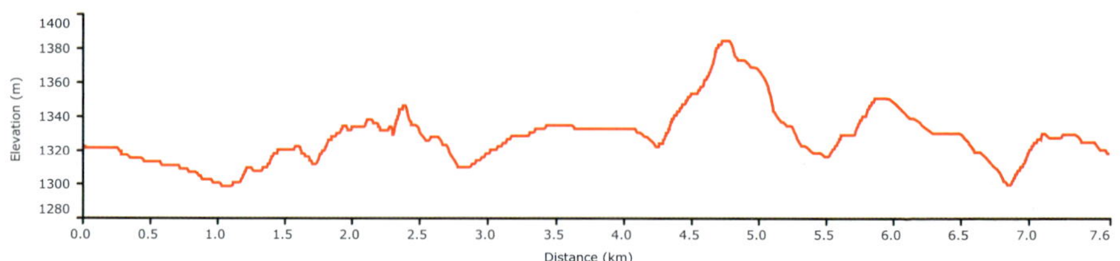

# 17 | RAZORS EDGE | 💀💀💀💀💀

| | |
|---|---|
| Distance: 5.1 km (current) | Technical Rating: Expert |
| Time: 1 - 2 hrs | Physical Rating: Hard |
| Elevation Gain: 167 m | Season: June - October |
| Elevation Loss: 492 m | Trail Type: All-Mountain |

Razors Edge is an incredible trail with stellar views and exciting terrain that puts it in a class of its own. Razors Edge is like no other ride in the Kananaskis Country. It's a BIG all mountain trail that utilizes the distinct and rugged terrain found in Quaite Valley. Accessible via Quaite Valley and Prairie View, Razors starts innocently enough. The first section of undulating singletrack running along a bench cut is one of the easier sections to navigate on this ride. Ascending gradually out of the thick forest and up to the first of many ridge lines, the trail only gets more intense. On the way up you'll be greeted with short, but steep, sections of slab while climbing and descending. Once on the ridge, the riding gets very technical. The narrow sections of ridge made up of rock, boulders and slab will keep one on their toes, while the descents down the longer sections of slab foretell of the riding yet to come.

What makes this ride so unique is the final section of exposed, steep and open ridge which will take you down lengthy sections of slab towards the highway. Expect long and steep sections of slab and in some cases very loose rocks. Incredible views of the surrounding mountains and valley below make this ride not only scenic, but spectacular. The trail builder has really nailed it with this trail, offering something for the more advanced rider that currently does not compare to any other rides in the Quaite Valley.

**IMPORTANT:** Razors Edge has received preliminary approval from Parks and once the proposed 1 km extension – connecting the ending of Razors Edge with Quaite Valley Connector – is constructed, the trail will become officially sanctioned. For now, please ride this trail at your own risk and be very careful when riding the highway shoulder back to Quaite Valley trail, a distance of approximately 1 km.

## TRAILHEAD | N51 02.563 W115 05.409

Park at the Heart Creek Day Use Area, located off Hwy 1 (TransCanada). Ride east along Quaite Valley Connector to Quaite Valley. Take a right (south) up Quaite Valley until you hit the Prairie View and Jewell Pass junction. Continue on up Prairie View for about 450 m to the trailhead for Razors Edge on your left, heading north.

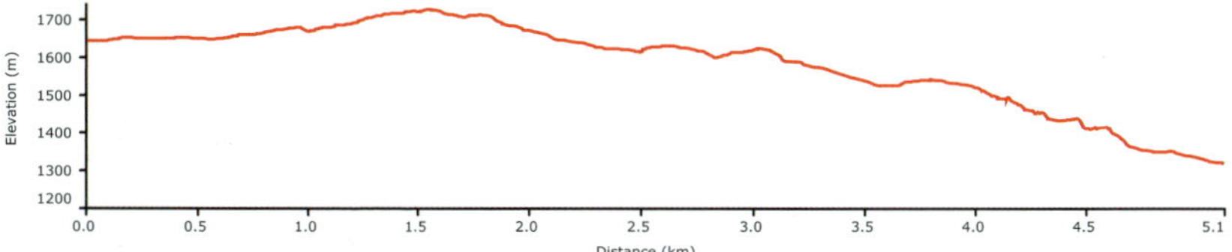

bikepirate✖com
bikepirate✖com
MAP 4: MOOSE MOUNTAIN
N
Moose Mountain
Moose Mountain Trail
Tom Snow
Moosepackers
Ridgeback
Tom Snow
Ranger Creek
Special K
Moose Mountain Rd.
T-Dub
SHAFT
Jean Guy
Slim SLEF
Toothless
Race of Spades
Diamond T Loop
Station Flats
66
Canyon Creek
BCT
Billy Dog
Pneuma
Sulphur Springs
66
Elbow River
Canyon Creek Road
Family Guy
Hot Laps
Elbow Valley
Prairie Mountain
Husky Road (Closed)
Ing's Mine
Brakeless
to Bragg Creek / Calgary
Elbow Valley
Riverview Trail
Moose Mountain Rd.
Parking
Powderface
2286
2134
1829
1829
1829
2134
1829
1676
1981
1829
1676
1829
1524
1676
1524
1524
1676
1524
1524
TransCanada Highway 1
Paved Road/Highway
Dirt Road
Trailhead
Water
Height in metres (m)
1800
Trail Junction
Beginner Trails
Intermediate Trails
Advanced / Expert Trails
Camping
Toilets / Outhouse
Parking
1 km
SCALE

# MOOSE MOUNTAIN

Located near Bragg Creek and about 45 minutes west of Calgary, Moose Mountain is a mountain biker's play land. Boasting an abundance of downhill and x-country trails ranging in difficulty from beginner to expert, this area has enough riding to keep you busy for a couple of days.

Downhill trails in the area include Technical Trail Features (TTFs) such as wooden structures, drops and gaps. They range from steep and gnarly descents down fall lines to flowy and smooth switchbacks with perfectly bermed corners to test your bike handling prowess. Most downhill trails were originally built by dedicated riders/builders, but development of new trails and maintenance has since come under the stewardship of Moose Mountain Bike Trail Society (MMBTS), a volunteer-based organization.

The x-country singletrack trails in the area vary from winding singletrack climbs and descents to fire roads and doubletracks. All the new x-country trails in the area, including Pneuma and Ridgeback, have been built to traverse and flow along the landscape. Ridgeback is looked after by the Calgary Mountain Bike Alliance (CMBA), while Pneuma was built by and is the responsibility of the MMBTS. MMBTS's mandate is to maintain and grow the existing network of downhill and x-country trails located on Moose Mountain.

If you're into riding a big bike on trails accessible by a shuttle vehicle or looking to pedal your all-mountain/x-country rig up some winding and technical singletrack, then Moose Mountain is the place for you. With all the area has to offer, you are sure to come back over and over again. Please note the seasonal road closure. Moose Mountain Road is closed annually to vehicles from December 1 - May 15.

### TRAILHEAD | N50.89947 W114.70112 (STATION FLATS); N50.8729403 W114.722886 (MOOSE MTN. RD.); N50.87331 W114.75560 (ING'S MINE)

From Bragg Creek take Hwy 22 south, turning west (right) on to Hwy 66. Drive west past McLean Creek and a short distance past Station Flats. About 2.8 km past Station Flats look for Moose Mountain Rd., located on the north side (right) of Hwy 66. The road is all gravel with a small parking area located at the bottom, next to the Pneuma trailhead. All downhill trails are accessed via Moose Mountain Road. If you're riding x-country then you may want to park at Station Flats, depending on the trail(s) you decide to ride.

# 18 | BRIDGE CONNECTOR TRAIL (BCT)

BCT serves one purpose: to provide access across Canyon Creek during the spring and early summer when water levels in the creek run high. The trail runs from the bottom of Billy Dog to the end of SHAFT/T-Dub, providing Moose Mountain's west side trails access to a manmade wooden bridge crossing Canyon Creek. The bridge is located where T-Dub finishes. A BIG thank you to the MMBTS and volunteers who built the bridge. Use BCT when water levels are high and crossing the creek may be too dangerous.

# 19 | BRAKELESS | 💀 💀 💀

| | |
|---|---|
| Distance: 1.8 km | Technical Rating: Beginner |
| Time: 10 - 20 min | Physical Rating: Easy |
| Elevation Gain: 15 m | Season: May - October |
| Elevation Loss: 175 m | Trail Type: Downhill |

Brakeless is one of three beginner downhill trails located on Moose Mountain; the others are Hot Laps and the considerably longer Family Guy. A short 70-m push up the first section of this trail gets you to the start of the downhill. The first section of the down is slightly fast and steep, with a number of bermed corners. This section ends as quickly as it begins and is followed by a very gentle rolling grade that will take you all the way down to the end of the trail, exiting onto Hwy 66. From there one can pedal left (east) to the start of Moose Mountain Road to meet up with your shuttle and do this run all over again, or head right (west) to the Ing's Mine parking lot to meet up with your shuttle buddies there.

There are no Technical Trail Features (TTFs) found on Brakeless, other than the bermed corners and a small half-a-foot hop at the end of the short and slightly steep bit. This is a great run to take your kids on for a spin or a good run for somebody new to the sport looking to try downhill riding.

## TRAILHEAD | N50 52.764 W114 44.956

The trailhead is located a short 2.4 km shuttle or pedal up from the bottom of Moose Mountain Road. Look for a large parking area on your left at about the 2.4 km mark. Park and look for the well-marked trailhead heading off into the woods and starting with a short uphill push.

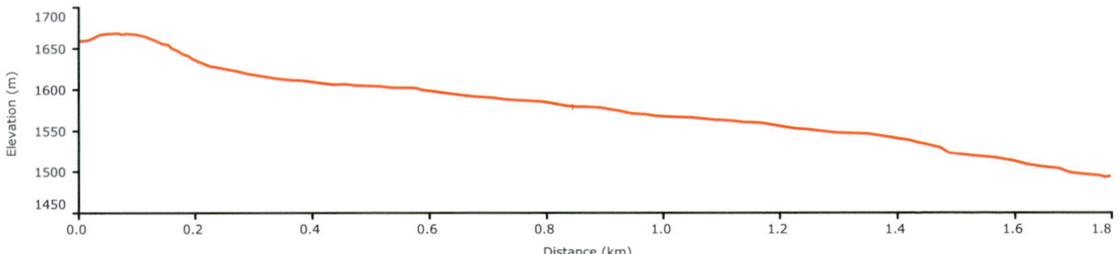

# 20 | FAMILY GUY | ☠ ☠ ☠ ☠

**Distance: 4.8 km**
**Time: 15 - 45 min**
**Elevation Gain: 40 m**
**Elevation Loss: 460 m**

**Technical Rating: Beginner - Intermediate**
**Physical Rating: Moderate**
**Season: June - October**
**Trail Type: Downhill**

Family Guy is a beginner/intermediate trail located on the west side of Moose Mountain. It may be used as a connector to SLF, Toothless and Billy Dog, some of the more advanced trails on Moose Mountain, or is best ridden on its own. This is a great introductory trail to the offerings on Moose Mountain and one of the longest descents on the west side of the mountain. The construction of Family Guy trail has been made possible by the hard efforts of nearly 200 dedicated volunteers, including many family groups, inspiring the Family Guy name.

The trailhead is located on the west side of Moose Mountain Road, just below Jean Guy and the carpark. It starts down a wonderful set of very well laid-out stones onto a sweet and mellow singletrack. The trail pops in and out of the aspen and pine trees, offering up some incredible views of the surrounding mountains and valley below. The aspen trees are a special treat during the fall when the colours start to turn, making for truly incredible scenery. The trail has some great flow, a few tighter sections through the trees and some wide open sections that can be found along the bench heading down to Ing's Mine.

At this time, the trail is only open until it reaches Billy Dog. Beyond Billy Dog, Family Guy is closed and still under construction. Please respect the closure until the completion of the trail. The MMBTS hopes to complete final leg of the trail in early spring 2013.

## TRAILHEAD | N50 54.622 W114 45.894

The trailhead for Family Guy is well marked and can be found a 100 m south of the Jean Guy Trailhead on Moose Mountain Road. Park at the Jean Guy pull-off on Moose Mountain Road and ride 100 m back down Moose Mountain, looking for the trailhead on the rider's right on the west side of Moose Mountain Road.

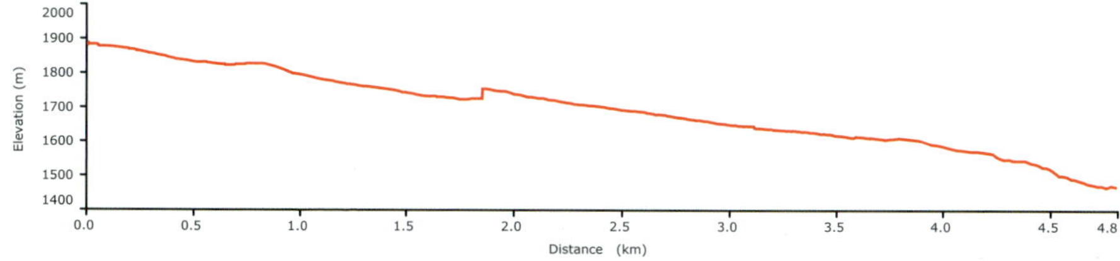

# 21 | HOT LAPS | ☠

| | |
|---|---|
| Distance: 1.3 km | Technical Rating: Beginner |
| Time: 5 - 15 min | Physical Rating: Easy |
| Elevation Gain: 8 m | Season: June - October |
| Elevation Loss: 86 m | Trail Type: Downhill |

Hot Laps is a downhill trail built for the beginner rider. A part of the Moose Mountain trail network, Hot Laps has seen better days and is in need of some TLC. It has become overgrown and hard to follow, due to the lack of traffic. Hot Laps used to be the only option for beginner downhill riders, but now there are Brakeless and Family Guy, both of which are well maintained and a lot more fun to ride. In my humble opinion, Hot Laps is only worth riding if you're looking to say that you've done it.

Hot Laps is a low angle trail, with no Technical Trail Features (TTFs) to worry about. It is one hundred percent singletrack all the way down to Elbow Valley trail, which runs perpendicular to it. Cross Elbow Valley and continue on down Pneuma to spit out at the bottom of Moose Mountain Road. When blasting down Pneuma, watch out for riders pedaling up. Pneuma is a popular x-country trail providing access to several trails on Moose Mountain.

## TRAILHEAD | N50 53.005 W114 45.122

Access Hot Laps via Moose Mountain Road. Drive 2.8 km up Moose Mountain Road and look for the trailhead to your right, on the east side of the road. It is clearly marked, but sometimes hard to spot when driving your vehicle.

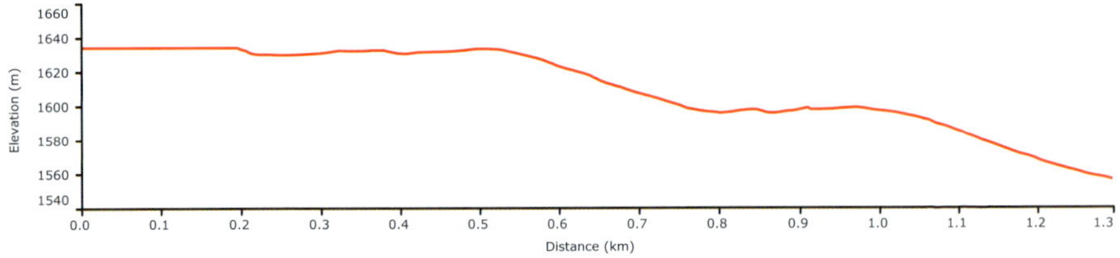

# 22 | RACE OF SPADES | ☠ ☠ ☠ ☠ ☠

| | |
|---|---|
| Distance: 5.8 km (to Station Flats) | Technical Rating: Intermediate |
| Time: 30 min – 1.5 hrs | Physical Rating: Moderate |
| Elevation Gain: 64 m | Season: June - October |
| Elevation Loss: 543 m | Trail Type: Downhill |

Race of Spades is one of the longer downhill tracks located on Moose Mountain and a favourite amongst the locals. It is a great run well suited to intermediate and expert riders alike. The trail starts with a few short, tight, and steep sections, but overall is a moderate grade ride down to the Station Flats parking area. There are numerous Technical Trail Features (TTFs) on Race of Spades, ranging from intermediate to expert in difficulty. All TTFs do have a ride-around option for the less experienced rider.

A short but steep hike-a-bike section is found about 2.4 km down the trail – it's 200 m in length. The climb begins right after the long TTF consisting of a ladder connecting to a skinny log ride which features a teeter, thrown in to test your balance and bike handling skills. Following the short climb is more descending through tights trees that take you to larger TTFs (gap jumps), all with ride-around options. The trail does split at one point, providing the rider two options; both meet up a few hundred metres down the trail. The option to the rider's right consists of two gap and table top jumps, both side by side, followed by a short wall ride. The option down the fall line (left) takes the rider over large TTFs and continues on down the trail to where the two options eventually merge. Finally, the trail spits you out on a doubletrack, just after you complete the short pump track section through the trees. Keep right at the junctions, cross the bridge, head up the mini hill, and follow the doubletrack out to the Station Flats parking area.

## TRAILHEAD | N50 54.705 W114 45.994 (TH); N50 53.732 W114 42.326 (STATION FLATS)

Drive up Moose Mountain Road to the pull-off for Jean Guy on your left. Park and ride back down the road for about 100 m to the entrance for Race of Spades . You will spot a singletrack trail to the rider's left across the ditch running parallel to the road for about 30 m before it drops into the trees. A map and sign indicating the start of Race of Spades are clearly visible from Moose Mountain Road, marking the trailhead.

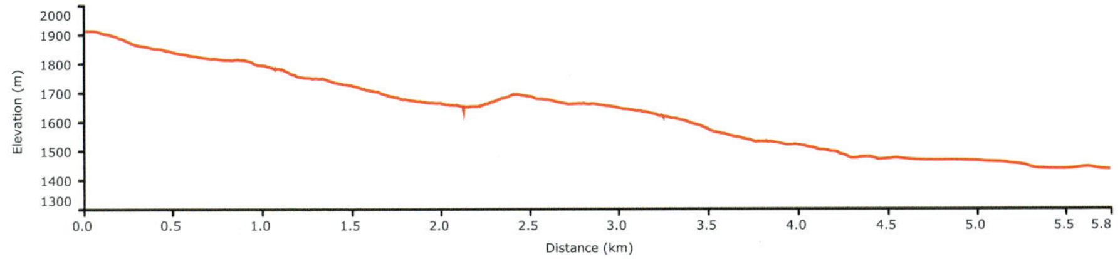

# 23 | SHAFT | 💀 💀 💀 💀

| | |
|---|---|
| Distance: 3.3 km | Technical Rating: Intermediate |
| Time: 30 min – 1 hr | Physical Rating: Easy |
| Elevation Gain: 21 m | Season: June - October |
| Elevation Loss: 457 m | Trail Type: Downhill |

SHAFT is an acronym that stands for Super Happy Awesome Fun Trail. This trail is just that – super fun! Built with the beginner to intermediate rider in mind, SHAFT is now the longest downhill trail located on Moose Mountain. Different from trails like T-Dub or Jean-Guy, this trail is all about the flow; no manmade structures are to be found on this trail. You can really get your groove on as you glide down the smooth switchbacks and utilize the bermed corners to carry your speed down the trail.

SHAFT is a great trail to use when introducing beginner to intermediate riders to downhill riding, as it will help them build the skills and confidence required to ride the more advanced trails on Moose Mountain. It is a part of the Moose Mountain trail network and is the first completely new trail built by MMBTS.

## TRAILHEAD | N50 54.843 W114 46.730

Drive up Moose Mountain Road to the gate at the top. From there pedal past the gate, up the hill, and over to T-Dub - 200 m from the gate. The trailhead to SHAFT is right next to T-Dub and heads right, down the side of the hill.

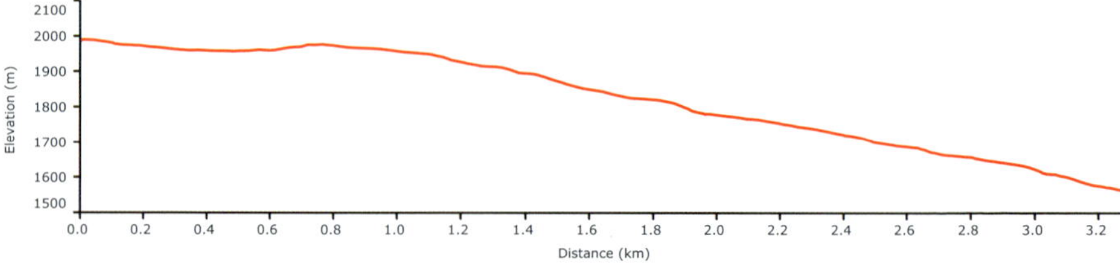

# 24 | BILLY DOG | ☠☠☠☠☠

| | |
|---|---|
| Distance: 1.4 km | Technical Rating: Advanced |
| Time: 5 - 20 min | Physical Rating: Moderate |
| Elevation Gain: 0 m | Season: June - October |
| Elevation Loss: 229 m | Trail Type: Downhill |

Billy Dog is yet another fun and challenging advanced (black) downhill run located on Moose Mountain, near Bragg Creek. I like to use this one as a warm up. It is a shorter run, with intermediate to expert Technical Trail Features (TTFs) peppering the bottom half of this trail. Located on the left side of Moose Mountain Road and well-marked by a signed trailhead, this trail takes to you to the Ing's Mine parking area. A word of caution, though: Billy Dog is not the best trail to ride in early spring or after heavy rains, as it contains several low points that pool water and become extremely muddy.

Billy Dog starts with a steep line to two options – steep and steeper – before the first TTF, a wooden drop. Following this section you'll continue on down some more switchbacking, steep and tight singletrack, before coming to a clearing in the trees. The first large TTF, a gap jump, followed by a smaller gap, is straight ahead. Make sure to check the TTF before you leap and to gage your speed to clear it. From this point the trail heads back into the woods, with several more TTFs along Billy Dog until the end of the trail. The last section contains a few more short, but steep, downs that demand respect as a fall here would see you land further away from your bike than you might find comfortable.

Once you pop out at the bottom of the trail, there are two options to get across Canyon Creek. If the creek is running high, head right, taking BCT trail to connect with the wooden bridge built to cross the creek.  If the creek is running low or if it's dry, then ride straight across it. Remember to pedal left, once you cross the creek, to get back to the Ing's Mine parking area.

## TRAILHEAD | N50 53.842 W114 45.107

Drive about 4.2 km up Moose Mountain Road to the trailhead located on the left hand side of the road. It's not the easiest trail to spot, so start looking for it after driving 4 km. There is small pull-off on the right side of the road to park, but again, if no one is parked there it is not that obvious. If you find yourself driving past the trailhead for Toothless and SLF, you've gone too far.

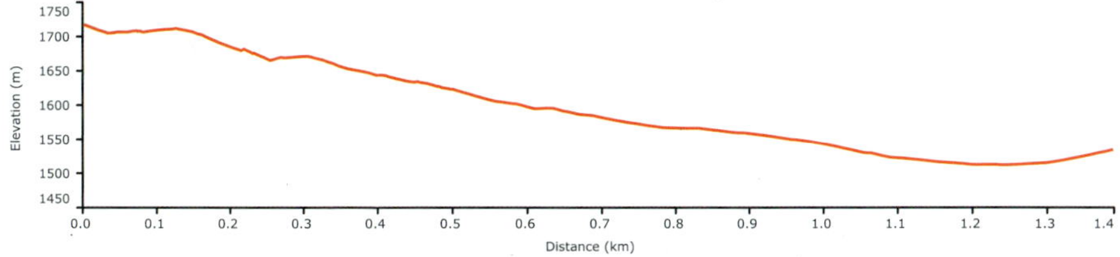

# 25 | JEAN GUY ON THE ROCKS | 💀💀💀💀💀

| | |
|---|---|
| Distance: 2.2 km | Technical Rating: Advanced |
| Time: 15 - 45 min | Physical Rating: Moderate |
| Elevation Gain: 0 m | Season: May - October |
| Elevation Loss: 401 m | Trail Type: Downhill |

Jean Guy On The Rocks is a downhiller's delight. A combination of steep trail with rock drops and man-made features will keep you engaged all the way down the trail. The first section is steep and narrow, followed by a rock drop and a manmade stunt. A third of the way down the trail the trees open up a little and the steep grade eases off. More stunts wait to test your bike handling skills – and in some cases your sanity. The second part of the trail joins up with SLF, where you will come across a gap jump followed by a large step up and a HUGE gap jump with a limited landing area.

If you like natural features, gap jumps and step ups, this trail is for you. Almost all the features have a ride-around option, aside from one at the beginning of the trail: a large rock roll, down a short section of wooden ladder. The trail ends with some sweet berms and a couple of table tops.

This is a great trail to ride early spring and late fall, as it dries out quickly because of its southwestern exposure.

## TRAILHEAD | N50 54.688 W114 45.978

The trailhead is located at 6.5 km on the west side of Moose Mountain Road, right next to the pull-off. It is well marked and begins with a short 20 m hike-a-bike section.

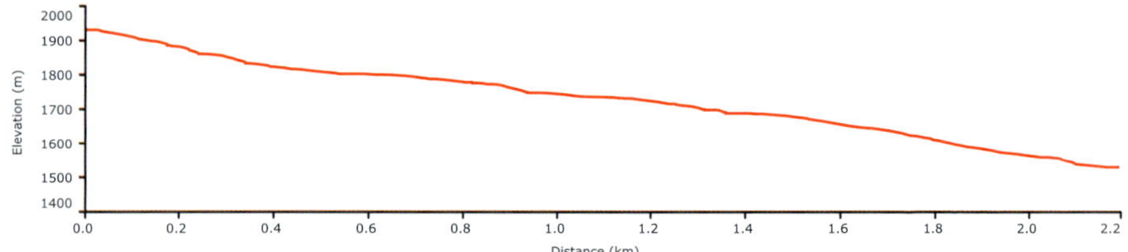

# 26 | SPECIAL K | 💀 💀 💀

**Distance:** 8 km (to Station Flats)
**Time:** 45 min - 1.5 hrs
**Elevation Gain:** 97 m
**Elevation Loss:** 652 m

**Technical Rating:** Advanced
**Physical Rating:** Hard
**Season:** May - October
**Trail Type:** Downhill/ All-Mountain

Special K is a classic downhill trail better suited to an all-mountain bike than a downhill, due to its length and the long ride out on Tom Snow. But don't be fooled – there are plenty of sections at the beginning to keep you on your toes, making this an advanced to expert ride in many of the spots encountered on the descents.

The trail measures 4.7 km to where it meets with Tom Snow. From there you'll have to climb up a long, steep hill, before descending back down and pedaling over to the Station Flats parking lot. The total distance is 8 km from the Special K trailhead.

You'll find there is no time to warm up on this trail, as it begins with a steep descent onto a large Technical Trail Feature (TTF) – probably the biggest on the trail. Not to worry, you do have an option to ride around the TTF. More steep descents intertwined with short mellow sections form this trail, which criss-crosses a stream bed over a number of wooden bridges. Expect about three manmade drops (TTFs) and loads of short, but steep, sections to keep things exciting. The final pedal out can be strenuous if you're riding a big bike, especially on a hot summer day, so bring lots of water for this ride.

## TRAILHEAD | N50 54.899 W114 46.236

Drive up Moose Mountain Road for about 6.8 km and look for the pipeline station perched on the right side of the hill. The trail starts next to the station shack. Drive to the end of the road to park if you're dropping a vehicle and pedal back down to the trailhead. Special K will spit you back out at Station Flats; leave a retrieval vehicle there.

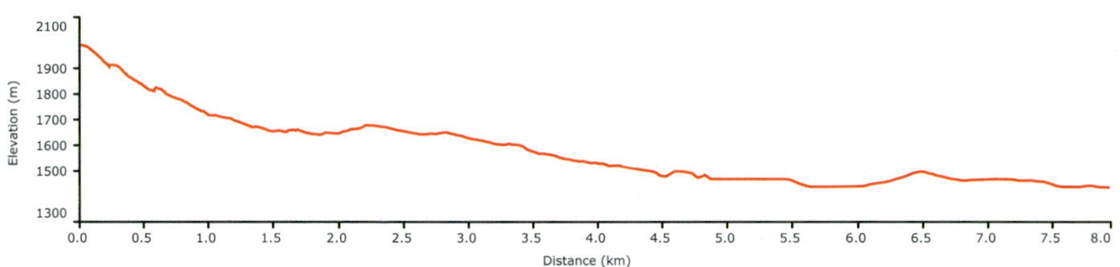

# 27 | T-DUB | 💀💀💀💀💀

| | |
|---|---|
| Distance: 2.5 km | Technical Rating: Advanced – Expert |
| Time: 30 min – 1 hr | Physical Rating: Moderate |
| Elevation Gain: 0 m | Season: June - October |
| Elevation Loss: 454 m | Trail Type: Downhill |

T-Dub combines technical steeps with plenty of rocks and an abundance of roots for one hell of a descent. Manmade and natural trail features are scattered all the way down the trail. Expect some large drops, massive roll downs and big rocks.

In 2008, a re-route of the Balboa gully section was completed to enhance the trail's sustainability. This option runs along the left side of the hill in a constant but flowy state. To avoid the gully and ride the re-route keep left, after crossing the first meadow. For those looking to experience a bit more gnar and wanting to hit the new jump line at the end of the gully, with the optional "whale tail" TTF, ride right down the gully entrance. The end of the gully meets up again at the entrance to the second meadow. From there stay left on the original line if you want something more mellow (intermediate) to get you to the end of the trail. Or head right, back into the trees, again to a jump line with several drops, step-up, bridge table, and wallride options. The choice of which route to take depends on your experience and comfort level hitting large TTFs.

## TRAILHEAD | N50 54.842 W114 46.728

T-Dub begins at the top of Moose Mountain Road. Leave a shuttle retrieval at Ing's Mine parking area. Drive up Moose Road and park just before the gate. The trailhead is 200 m past the gate on your left, right next to the SHAFT trailhead.

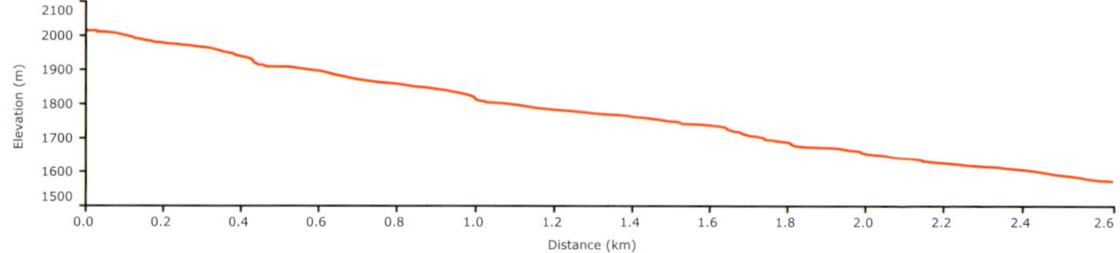

# 28 | TOOTHLESS | 💀 💀 💀

| | |
|---|---|
| Distance: 1.8 km | Technical Rating: Advanced |
| Time: 8 - 15 min | Physical Rating: Moderate |
| Elevation Gain: 9 m | Season: June - October |
| Elevation Loss: 328 m | Trail Type: Downhill |

Toothless is an advanced downhill run located on Moose Mountain. It starts off innocently enough – a flat section with a short up – before you're thrown full bore into it. The first Technical Trail Feature (TTF) is a filter for the trail; if you're not comfortable riding it, best continue down Family Guy. Tight and twisting turns with a number of berms to keep your flow and check your speed make this a thrilling descent. About two minutes down the trail, hit the small jump (use caution and check your speed) that will throw you into the start of the gnarly steep section of trail. Hang on to your bike here. The steep section takes you down loose dirt and jagged rock, while you pick up speed due to the extreme steepness. There is a ride-around built to avoid this section altogether, so if you don't like getting your butt sucked into your rear wheel, take the ride-around for a smoother run. Once past the super steep section, you'll encounter more loose rock and a TTF before riding out a monstrous steep berm and the remainder of the trail to the creek bed at the bottom. From there it's a 10-minute pedal back to Ing's Mine parking lot.

## TRAILHEAD | N50 54.344 W114 45.626

Access Toothless via Moose Mountain Road. Drive 5.5 km up Moose Mountain Road and look for the trailhead to your left, on the west side of the road. It is clearly marked, with a pull-off in front of it, next to Toothless is the trailhead for SLF.

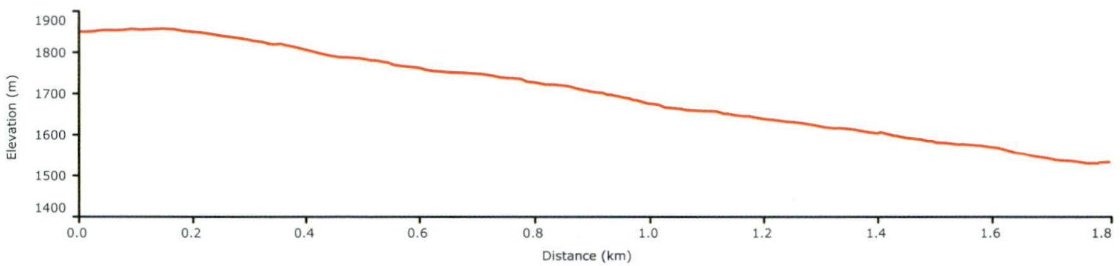

# 29 | SLF | 

| | |
|---|---|
| Distance: 1.4 km | Technical Rating: Expert |
| Time: 5 - 15 min | Physical Rating: Moderate |
| Elevation Gain: 0 m | Season: June - October |
| Elevation Loss: 321 m | Trail Type: Downhill |

SLF – which stands for Satan's Little Fluffers, an appropriate name for this trail – is an expert downhill run located on Moose Mountain. If you like steep, rocky sections with Technical Trail Features (TTFs) thrown in to spice things up, then you'll love this trail. All TTFs found on SLF are for the advanced to expert rider; don't even try riding them unless you've got the skill. The consequences of missing a gap or rolling off a skinny ladder are high on this trail. Now that you've been warned, those with the skill set will love the elevated TTFs, jumps and steep rocky bits. SLF is definitely one of the harder trails found on Moose Mountain.

The trail is broken up into two sections, upper SLF and lower SLF, providing an option out of the lower part of SLF altogether if you find yourself in over your head. Upper SLF meets up with Jean Guy and continues down it for about 280 m. You can choose to ride out on Jean Guy to complete your run, or continue down SLF. The access to lower SLF is located to your right as you pop out of the woods into a small clearing. Jean Guy will continue straight ahead back into the trees, while lower SLF will head right.

## TRAILHEAD | N50 54.348 W114 45.633

Access SLF via Moose Mountain Road. Drive 5.5 km up Moose Mountain Road and look for the trailhead to your left, on the west side of the road. It is clearly marked, with a pull-off in front of it. Next to SLF is the trailhead to Toothless.

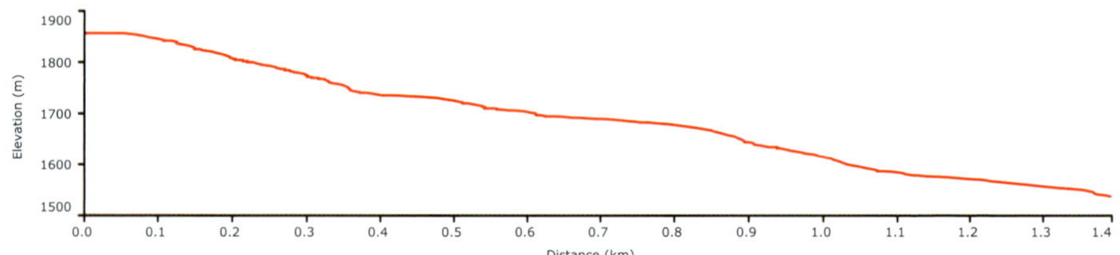

# 30 | MOOSE MOUNTAIN TRAIL | 💀 💀 💀

| | |
|---|---|
| Distance: 14 km (return) | Technical Rating: Beginner |
| Time: 1.5 - 3 hrs | Physical Rating: Moderate - Hard |
| Elevation Gain: 565 m | Season: July - October |
| Elevation Loss: 565 m | Trail Type: X-Country |

Moose Mountain Trail, also referred to as the Fire Lookout, is a gravel doubletrack that leads to the Fire Lookout point perched on the side of a massive cliff on the summit of Moose Mountain. Bikes are not allowed past the 7 km mark, so if you would like to get a better view from the top of the world, you'll have to hike it the last km to the top. I should add that the hike is well worth doing, especially on a clear day, as the views are incredible. Don't forget to bring your camera for this ride.

The trail offers some stunning 360 degree views of the surrounding mountain peaks and on a clear day one can easily see the City of Calgary to the east. There is nothing technical about this ride, other than the final 2 km grunt up a loose gravel doubletrack which switchbacks up the side of the mountain all the way to the summit. An out-and-back trail, Moose Mountain Trail may also be used as a connector to Moosepackers. The trailhead for Moosepackers is found 1.3 km down the trail just before you start the gradual climb up Moose Mountain Trail.

## TRAILHEAD | N50 54.924 W114 46.600 (PARKING); N50 54.925 W114 46.573 (TH)

To access the Moose Mountain Trail, take Hwy 66 west from Bragg Creek to Moose Mountain Road. Drive up to the top of Moose Mountain Road, a gravel road, and park close to the first gate in the Fire Lookout parking area. Moose Mountain Trail is marked with a large sign about 200 m up the trail, just beyond the gate located on the east side of Moose Mountain Road. A second gate at the end of Moose Mountain Road provides access to T-Dub and SHAFT – hardcore rides that are not where you want to head accidentally or casually!

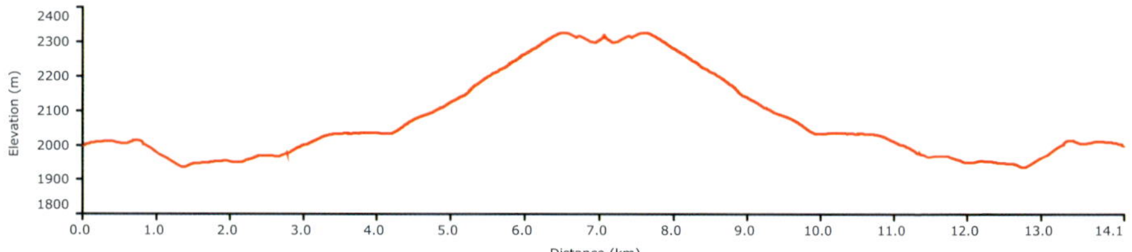

# 31 | DIAMOND T LOOP | 

| | |
|---|---|
| Distance: 4.1 km | Technical Rating: Intermediate |
| Time: 30 min - 1 hr | Physical Rating: Moderate |
| Elevation Gain: 144 m | Season: June - October |
| Elevation Loss: 142 m | Trail Type: X-Country |

Diamond T Loop is a short but fun loop which begins at the Station Flats parking area. It's a great trail to warm up on, or to help introduce a new rider to riding the variety of x-country trails located in the area. This is a multi-use trail that sees a lot of traffic on the weekends; please give way to hikers and pedestrians and watch out for downhill riders connecting up with Diamond T as they come off of Race of Spades, a downhill track.

Diamond T Loop flows wonderfully in either direction, so you decide which way to ride it. The trail is mainly doubletrack, mixed in with a few sections of wide singletrack. The trail will challenge the beginner rider, but the intermediate to advanced rider will find this one an easy pedal. A lookout point with views of the surrounding mountains and valley below offers a great rest spot worth checking out, about halfway down the trail. Other than a little bit of loose gravel on the west end of the loop when riding uphill and a creek crossing, there is nothing too exciting about this ride. This is exactly what a beginner pushing intermediate may prefer.

**TRAILHEAD | N50 53.513 W114 42.404 (CLOCKWISE); N50 53.714 W114 42.349 (COUNTER)**

From Bragg Creek, drive west along Hwy 66 to Station Flats. Park at Station Flats and look for the trailhead on the west end of the parking area; it's well marked. If riding it clockwise, follow Elbow Valley for a few hundred metres to the well-marked trailhead on the rider's right. Otherwise, follow the Diamond T Loop trailhead from Station Flats to ride it counter clockwise.

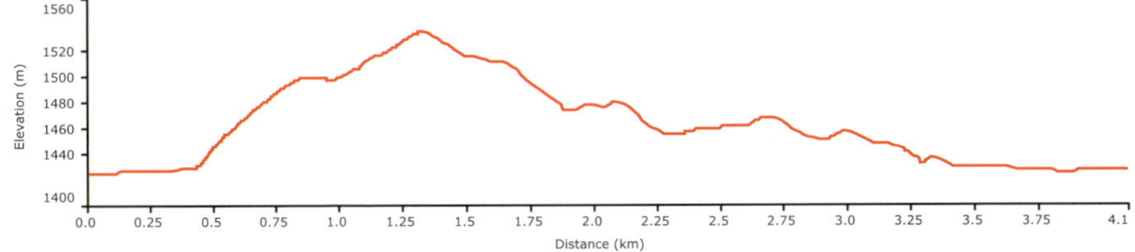

# 32 | MOOSEPACKERS | 

| | |
|---|---|
| Distance: 2.8 km | Technical Rating: Intermediate |
| Time: 10 - 30 min | Physical Rating: Easy |
| Elevation Gain: 55 m | Season: June - October |
| Elevation Loss: 332 m | Trail Type: X-Country |

Moosepackers is a classic trail that can be used as a climb or as a fast descent to connect with several other trails found in the area. When ridden as a descent, this trail is fast, flowy, and fun. It offers up several steep switchbacks for the rider to enjoy navigating down. Yet don't get too carried away shredding down the trail and make sure to stay in control. Moosepackers is very popular amongst hikers and several other trail users and does get busy during the summer months. Ride in control and give right-of-way to other trail users.

Moosepackers is primarily used to connect Pneuma with Tom Snow or with the recently built Ridgeback trail. My favourite route is to combine Pneuma with Moosepackers, taking Ridgeback down to Station Flats Day Use Area. From there I ride the short section of Hwy 66 west to Moose Mountain Road in order to retrieve my vehicle at the Pneuma trailhead.

**TRAILHEAD | N50 55.528 W114 46.730 (WEST TH); N50 55.555 W114 45.330 (EAST TH)**

To access the east end of the trail, park at Station Flats and ride north on Tom Snow for 5.4 km and look for the trail to the rider's left. To access the west end of the trail, ride up Pneuma until it spits you out on Moose Mountain Trail, just before the junction/trailhead for Moosepackers.

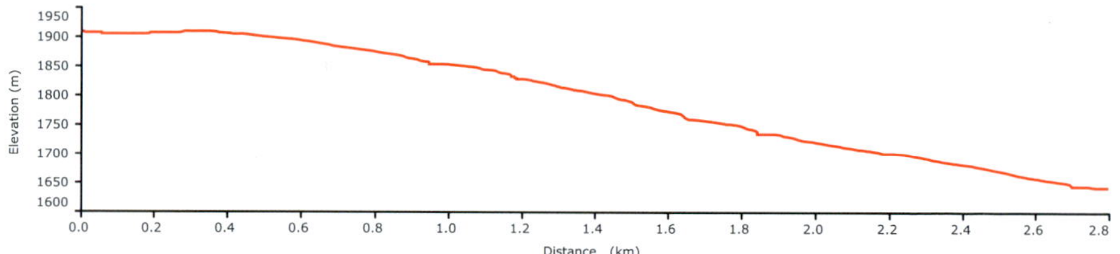

## 33 | PNEUMA | 💀 💀 💀

| | |
|---|---|
| Distance: 10.3 km | Technical Rating: Intermediate |
| Time: 1.5 - 2.5 hrs | Physical Rating: Moderate - Hard |
| Elevation Gain: 609 m | Season: June - October |
| Elevation Loss: 156 m | Trail Type: X-Country |

Pneuma is a relatively new singletrack trail built to provide access to the downhill and x-country trails found on Moose Mountain, and is a great alternative to pedaling up Moose Mountain Road. The trail leads to the end of Moose Mountain Road, continuing beyond until it connects up with Moose Mountain Trail just before the junction for Moosepackers. It may be ridden as an out-and-back or as a loop when combined with Moosepackers and Ridgeback. A beginner rider will find this trail a fun challenge, while the expert rider should enjoy the plethora of switchbacks as they make their way to the top.

The climb up Pnuema begins innocently enough, with a gradual grade twisting and winding its way up the hill. As you continue up the trail it gets considerably steeper and more technical, with the final km posing a challenge to even the more experienced rider. Keep an eye out for riders going the opposite way and remember that right-of-way goes to the downhill rider since it is harder for them to stop. Once you near the Race of Spades intersection, the well-worn trail crossing Pneuma about 7.8 km up trail, watch out for downhill riders barreling across the trail and yield at the junction to avoid a pile up.

### TRAIL OPTIONS

If you're looking for more of an all-mountain/downhill ride and don't have an extra vehicle to shuttle Moose Mountain Road, then climb Pneuma to the start of several downhill runs located on Moose. Combine it with any of the downhill trails in the area to complete an exhilarating loop. I would suggest climbing Pneuma to the end of Moose Mountain Road and taking SHAFT down to Ing's Mine, and from there pedaling along the road to the Pneuma trailhead.

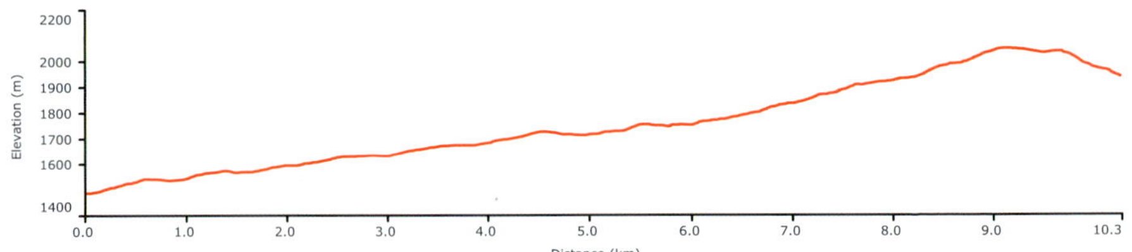

For the ultimate x-country loop, take Pneuma all the way to the start of Moosepackers. Moosepackers will connect you with Tom Snow and Ridgeback; choose either of these to get back to Station Flats. Tom Snow is the easier option if you're tired and don't want to extend your ride. However, Ridgeback is the better option for a sweeter ride. Plan about 2.5 to 4.5 hours when riding this loop (Pneuma – Moose Packers – Ridgeback).

## TRAILHEAD | N50 52.397 W114 43.437

Take Hwy 66 west from Bragg Creek to Moose Mountain Road. Turn right onto Moose Mountain Road and park your car in the parking area located at the turn off. Pneuma begins right from the carpark and is very well marked with a large trailhead sign.

# 34 | RIDGEBACK | 💀💀💀💀

Distance: 8.6 km (one way)
Time: 1.5 - 2.5 hrs
Elevation Gain: 197 m
Elevation Loss: 393 m

Technical Rating: Intermediate
Physical Rating: Moderate
Season: June - October
Trail Type: X-Country

Still a relatively unknown trail to most, the Ridgeback trail was built the fall of 2010 by CMBA with the help of a grant received from the Canadian Government. The trail is anything but boring. You'll find it twists, rolls, climbs and descends along a sweet tight singletrack. It may be ridden either direction – so watch out for oncoming traffic – and can also be ridden as an out-and-back or as a part of a loop. The trail criss-crosses Tom Snow in several spots, providing the rider an option to bail out from the trail via Tom Snow if short on time or running out of steam.

The great thing about Ridgeback is that it is a fun trail to ride on its own or even better when combined as a part of a loop. Loop this trail by starting your ride up Pneuma, over to Moosepackers and down Ridgeback, or ride up Tom Snow from Station Flats to descend back down Ridgeback. I personally find Ridgeback flows best when descended.

The trail stats provided are based on riding Ridgeback down from Moosepackers to Station Flats. If riding from Station Flats, expect twice the elevation gain and about an hour longer to ascend.

### TRAILHEAD | N50 54.049 W114 42.702 (MOOSEPACKERS)

Take Hwy 66 west of Bragg Creek to Station Flats Day Use Area. Park and ride out on Diamond T Loop/Tom Snow over to the Ridgeback trailhead. It is well marked at all intersections with a sign and trail map.

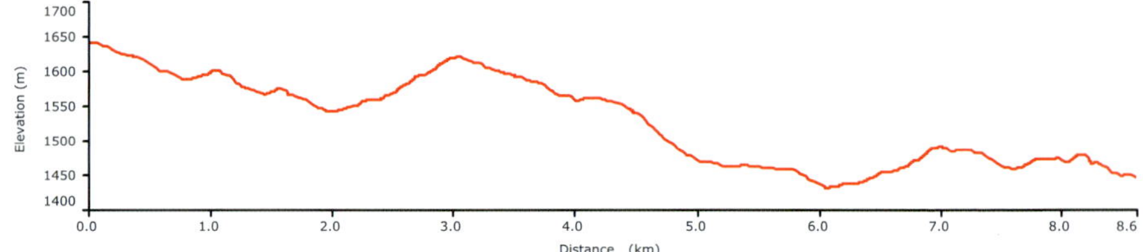

# 35 | RIVERVIEW TRAIL | 

| | |
|---|---|
| Distance: 4 km (one way) | Technical Rating: Intermediate |
| Time: 30 min - 1 hr | Physical Rating: Easy |
| Elevation Gain: 151 m | Season: June - October |
| Elevation Loss: 48 m | Trail Type: X-Country |

Riverview Trail is a scenic intermediate singletrack that may be ridden either direction and is accessed via the Paddy's Flat Recreation Area. The trail runs along the Elbow River and may be used to access the Sulphur Springs Trail and the Elbow Valley Trail for those staying at Paddy's Flat and wishing to do a longer x-country ride.

This is a scenic ride along the Elbow River with very little elevation gain and is a great trail for families to enjoy. The little bit of elevation – a short hill climb – on this trail takes you up to an amazing lookout on top of a ravine, offering some incredible views of the Elbow River below. Ride this trail as an out-and-back or as a connector trail; the choice is yours. If you decide to continue on the trail to Elbow Valley Trail, you will climb out onto Hwy 66, crossing the highway and continuing your climb up to the trailhead for both Sulphur Springs and Elbow Valley.  Both are well marked via a trail sign.

When riding Riverview Trail, please stay bear aware, as you are in bear country. Carry bear spray at all times. It is best to travel in groups and make lots of noise.

## TRAILHEAD | N50 52.597 W114 42.839

Drive west on Hwy 66 from Bragg Creek to the Paddy's Flat Recreation Area; if you don't have a reservation to camp, park at the gates or along the road. Ride to the trailhead located at the southeast end of the campground. The trailhead is well marked.

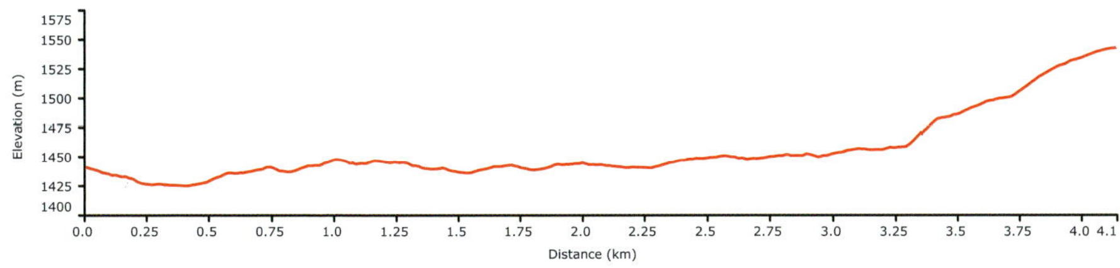

# 36 | TOM SNOW | 

| | |
|---|---|
| Distance: 29 km (one way) | Technical Rating: Intermediate |
| Time: 3 - 5 hrs | Physical Rating: Moderate |
| Elevation Gain: 522 m | Season: June - October |
| Elevation Loss: 580 m | Trail Type: X-Country |

Tom Snow serves as the main connector between Elbow Valley and Sibbald Area. It is not a very well maintained trail, but used heavily by equestrians and few mountain bikers. The trail winds through foothills east and north of Moose Mountain and may be ridden north to south or in reverse; you decide. There are a number of scenic sections along this mostly doubletrack trail; however, for the most part, this trail could use some work. Expect mud bogs and plenty of them, impassable in sections during the spring or after heavy rains. When the mud finally starts to dry, the trail can get very rough due to cattle and horse traffic.

Although there isn't a whole lot of elevation gained over the length of the trail, it is not one for the inexperienced backcountry mountain biker. Riding the 30 km leg from Dawson to Station Flats will have you navigating through deep sections of mud, crossing plenty of creeks, and jumping, or lifting, your bike over fallen trees. It is best to avoid this trail after heavy rain fall or during the spring time. If riding the full stretch, make sure you have a retrieval vehicle on the other end or someone waiting to pick you up as it's a long ride to do as an out-and-back, unless you enjoy that sort of thing.

Tom Snow may be used to connect the West Bragg Creek trail network with the Moose Mountain network or the Sibbald Area network of trails.

**TRAILHEAD | N51 01.431 W114 52.862 (DAWSON); N50 53.726 W114 42.333 (STATION)**

Dawson Recreation Area access: Take Hwy 68 (Sibbald Creek Trail) to Powderface Trail, a dirt road. Drive south on Powderface Trail about 5 km to the Dawson Equestrian Campground and Day Use area; it is well signed. The trailhead is well marked and begins at the northeast corner of the parking lot.

Station Flats access: From Bragg Creek drive west on Hwy 66 to the Station Flats turn-off; the turn-off is well signed. The trailhead is well marked and begins at the northwest corner of the carpark.

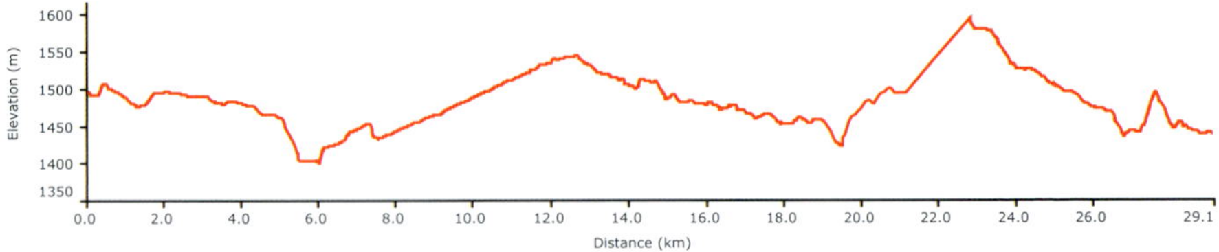

# 37 | ELBOW VALLEY | 💀 💀 💀

| | |
|---|---|
| Distance: 10.3 km (one way) | Technical Rating: Advanced |
| Time: 1 - 2 hrs | Physical Rating: Hard |
| Elevation Gain: 437 m | Season: June - October |
| Elevation Loss: 349 m | Trail Type: X-Country |

Elbow Valley is a challenging singletrack trail that takes you from Station Flats over to the Powderface Creek / Prairie Creek Loop. You can ride this singletrack either direction, loop it with Sulphur Springs or use it as a connector to the Powderface parking area.

Starting from Station Flats, follow the Elbow Valley trail west on the wide singletrack, passing by the Diamond T-loop turn-off to your right and the Sulphur Springs turn-off another few hundred metres thereafter. The trail begins to climb once you pass the Sulphur Springs trailhead. Expect long, steep, and loose climbs, followed with some sweet technical descents. The fast singletrack descents are tight and narrow, adding to the excitement of your ride. About halfway through the ride you will end up on a tight singletrack section that follows a cliff ban as you descend down to Ing's Mine Road. At the bottom of this descent, you will need to cross a creek (that typically runs dry) before popping out on Ing's Mine Road. Look for the well-marked trail continuing on into the woods, on the other side of the road. From there begin your climb up the trail, crossing the Husky Road, a gravel road, and making your way up to a small junction, not marked. Stay left and continue on all the way to the Powderface Day Use Area and parking lot. (If you choose right, you will continue to climb and eventually come to a dead end.)

## TRAILHEAD | N50 53.716 W114 42.333

From Bragg Creek drive west along Hwy 66 to Station Flats parking area. Park and look for the trailhead to Elbow Valley Trail on the west side of the carpark.

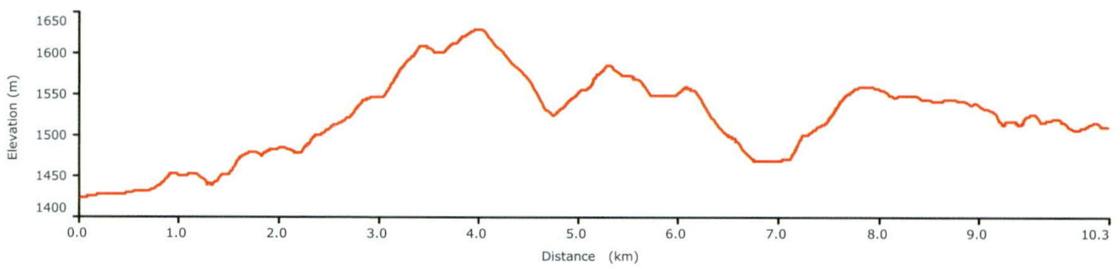

# 38 | SULPHUR SPRINGS LOOP | 💀💀💀💀

| | |
|---|---|
| Distance: 12.3 km | Technical Rating: Advanced |
| Time: 1 - 2 hours | Physical Rating: Hard |
| Elevation Gain: 472 m | Season: June - October |
| Elevation Loss: 455 m | Trail Type: X-Country |

Sulphur Springs Loop combines the well-known Sulphur Springs singletrack with Elbow Valley Trail to form a challenging technical ride that one can do after work or with limited time. A popular trail among mountain bikers and hikers, the loop may be ridden either direction. I prefer riding it counter clockwise starting up Sulphur Springs. If you want a challenge, ride the loop in reverse to find it flows completely differently.

To begin this loop, start at the Station Flats parking lot and look for the Elbow Valley trail located at the west end of the parking lot. Ride along the Elbow Valley trail for about 1 km before turning up the well-marked Sulphur Springs trail. The trail will begin to ascend for the next 4 km, winding its way through the forest up the tight doubletrack trail; the trail eventually narrows about halfway up, becoming a full on singletrack ride. Once you've completed the grunt up, you'll be rewarded with some great views of the surrounding mountains and valley below. Now comes the fun part. Taking a break from all the climbing, you'll get to barrel down (watch out for hikers) the fun and flowy singletrack descent taking you out to Elbow Valley Trail. Enjoy this exhilarating and fun rip down the last part of Sulphur Springs trail. Then, continue east (left) along Elbow Valley Trail all the way back to Station Flats. A heads up: the climbing is not over once back on Elbow Valley, as you'll be greeted with one very long grunt uphill before the trail starts to mellow out and descends back down to Station Flats.

### TRAILHEAD | N50 53.727 W114 42.337 (STATION FLATS); N50 53.163 W114 42.660 (TH)

Take Hwy 66 from Bragg Creek to the Station Flats parking area. Park and ride your bike, following the Elbow Valley trail, to the Sulphur Springs trailhead; it is about a km from the parking area.

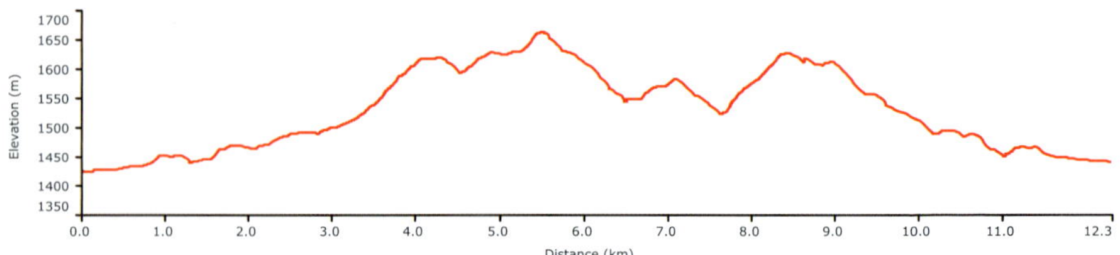

Ranger Summit

MAP 5: WEST BRAGG CREEK (NORTH TRAILS)
N
bikepirate✖com
bikepirate✖com
Telephone Loop (winter)
Long Distance
1524
1524
1524
1524
1524
1524
Tom Snow
Reconnect
Demi-Tel
Braggin Rights
Telephone Loop (summer)
Snowshoe Hare
1372
1372
All trails in this area are designated as multi-use. Please respect other trail users.

Telephone Loop (winter) and Snowshoe Hare are cross-country ski trails not maintained for summer use.
Bragg Creek
Township Rd. 232
to Bragg Creek / Calgary
West Bragg Creek Trailhead
West Bragg Creek (South Trails)
700 m
SCALE
TransCanada Highway 1
Paved Road/Highway
Dirt Road
Trailhead
Water
1800   Height in metres (m)
Trail Junction
Beginner Trails
Intermediate Trails
Advanced / Expert Trails
Camping
Toilets / Outhouse
Parking
Gate

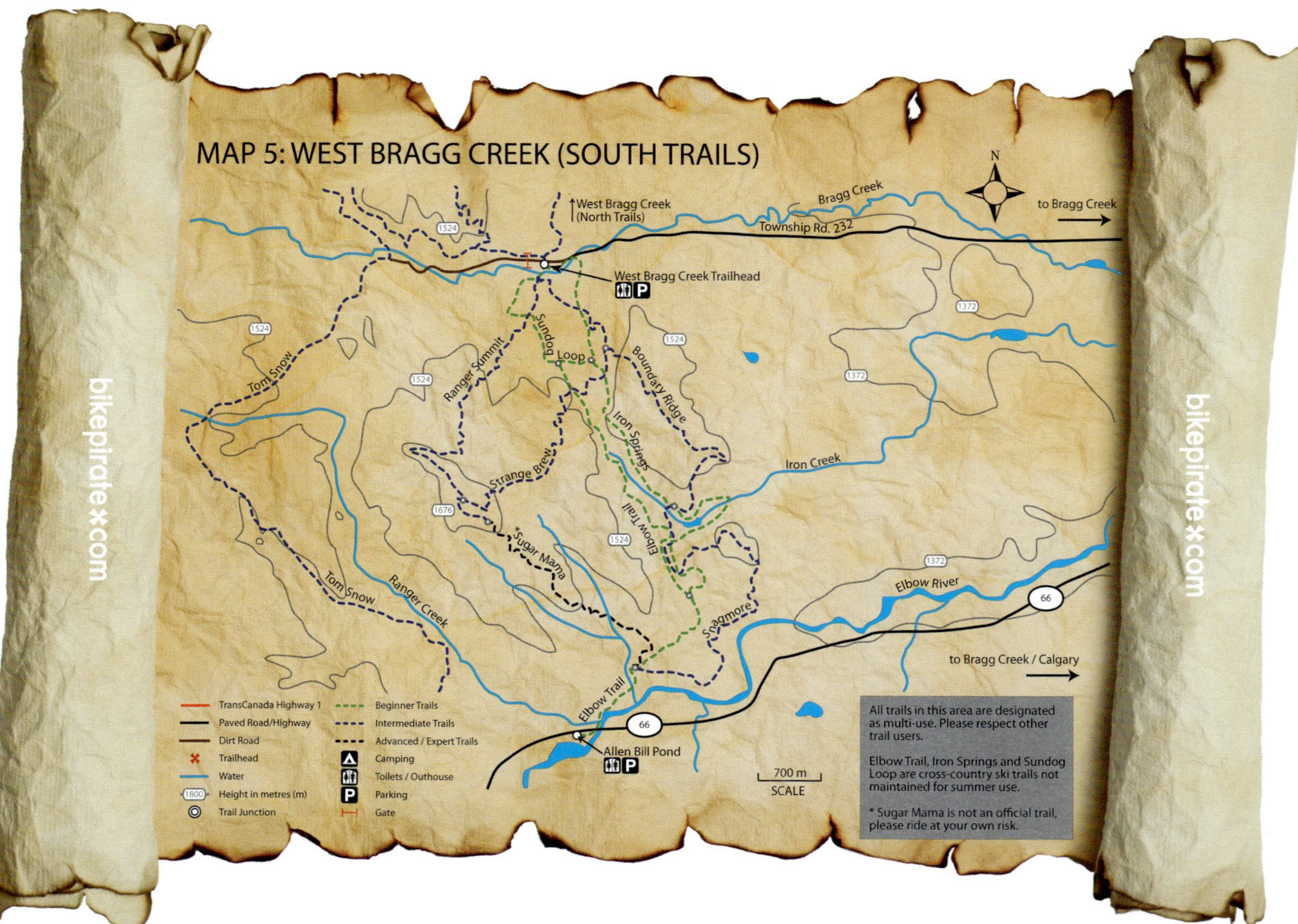

MAP 5: WEST BRAGG CREEK (SOUTH TRAILS)
N
bikepirate✶com
bikepirate✶com
Bragg Creek
to Bragg Creek
Township Rd. 232
West Bragg Creek (North Trails)
West Bragg Creek Trailhead
1524
1372
1524
1372
Tom Snow
Ranger Summit
Sundog Loop
Boundary Ridge
1524
Iron Springs
Iron Creek
Strange Brew
Iron Springs
Elbow Trail
1524
1676
*Sugar Mama
1372
Elbow River
66
Tom Snow
Ranger Creek
Snagmore
to Bragg Creek / Calgary
Elbow Trail
66
Allen Bill Pond
700 m
SCALE
TransCanada Highway 1
Paved Road/Highway
Dirt Road
Trailhead
Water
1800  Height in metres (m)
Trail Junction
Beginner Trails
Intermediate Trails
Advanced / Expert Trails
Camping
Toilets / Outhouse
Parking
Gate
All trails in this area are designated as multi-use. Please respect other trail users.
Elbow Trail, Iron Springs and Sundog Loop are cross-country ski trails not maintained for summer use.
* Sugar Mama is not an official trail, please ride at your own risk.

# WEST BRAGG CREEK

In 2011, over 33 km of intermediate, fast, and flowy singletrack trails were built in the West Bragg Creek area by the Greater Bragg Creek Trails Association, a purely volunteer group of Bragg Creek residents that are working hard to design, build and maintain trails and pathways for the benefit of residents and visitors of Bragg Creek. The trails are all multi-use and may be ridden in either direction, providing the rider with a plethora of loop options, including the Goldilocks, Southern Flow, and Northern Flow Loops. Riders are encouraged to be safe and show respect to other trail users as the popular trail network has seen significant rapid growth. All trails are well marked with trail markers and maps at major intersections, making it virtually impossible to get lost.

The West Bragg Creek summer trail network was developed by a unique collaboration amongst all user groups, including hikers, equestrians and mountain bikers. These volunteer groups have come together to help fundraise and build this incredible network of singletrack trails, adding to the already popular winter trail network. A huge thank you goes out to the Greater Bragg Creek Trails Association for all the effort this group has put into creating and maintaining these amazing trails. If you've not had the chance to explore the vast network of singletrack trails, only 45 minutes west of Calgary, then you're in for a treat.

## TRAILHEAD | N50 56.898 W114 41.584 (PARKING)

From Bragg Creek take Balsam Ave. west to Centre Ave. Turn southwest (left) at the T-junction on to Centre Ave. Drive southwest on Centre Ave., which will turn into Township Rd. 232. Continue on Township Rd. 232 until you hit the gravel road. Cross the cattle guard and drive to the well-marked parking area 500 m ahead on your right.

*Logging Alert! At the time of publishing this guidebook, logging recently modified by the Alberta Government is currently underway in the West Bragg Creek area and that logging will affect the newly built and existing trails. Please check www.bikepirate.com or http://braggcreektrails.org for updates and the latest information on the logging taking place before venturing out on the trails.*



bikepirate✖com

# 39 | DEMI-TEL | ☠

Distance: 1.6 km
Time: 10 - 30 min
Elevation Gain: 11 m
Elevation Loss: 100 m

Technical Rating: Beginner
Physical Rating: Easy
Season: June - October
Trail Type: X-Country

Demi-Tel is a short connector trail located on the north side of the West Bragg Creek Trails network. It connects Long Distance with Telephone Loop (summer section). To connect to Telephone Loop from Long Distance, ride Demi-Tel to Snowshoe Hare junction. At the junction turn left (east) and ride 700 m over to the summer portion of Telephone Loop. The Telephone Loop takes you back down (south) to the West Bragg Creek parking area. If you head north on Telephone Loop you will eventually come across the northern trailhead for Long Distance. Please note that the east leg of Telephone Loop is maintained for summer use, while the west leg, past the trailhead for Long Distance, is not.

Demi-Tel is a doubletrack trail with a few short sections of singletrack offering the rider little reward. The trail descends gradually over to Snowshoe Hare and is a quick ride in either direction. It is a beginner to intermediate ride built to connect with Telephone Loop and is not worth riding unless you're using it to return to the parking area via a shorter loop.

## TRAILHEAD | N50 57.626 W114 42.942

From Bragg Creek take Balsam Ave. west to Centre Ave. Turn southwest (left) at the T-junction on to Centre Ave. Drive southwest on Centre Ave., which will turn into Township Rd. 232. Continue on Township Rd. 232 until you hit the gravel road. Cross the cattle guard and drive to the well-marked parking area 500 m ahead on your right. Use Demi-Tel as a connector, accessing it via Long Distance or Snowshoe Hare Loop.

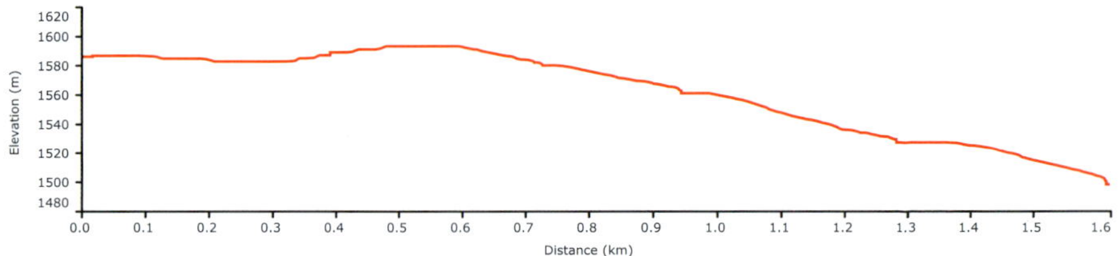

# 40 | ELBOW TRAIL | 

Distance: 5.7 km
Time: 45 min – 1.5 hrs
Elevation Gain: 152 m
Elevation Loss: 59 m

Technical Rating: Beginner
Physical Rating: Moderate
Season: June - October
Trail Type: X-Country

Elbow Trail is a wide doubletrack trail located in the West Bragg Creek Trails network and frequently used by equestrians. This popular winter x-country ski trail serves as a connector between all the new multi-use singletrack trails during the summer. You will want to avoid riding this trail in early spring and after heavy rains, which cause the trail to be less than desirable for mountain biking. Mud bogs and ruts make this trail a challenging one to navigate after a downpour.

Elbow Trail may be combined with Boundary Ridge or Snagmore, great singletrack trails worth checking out, for a quick loop depending on where you chose to park at the West Bragg Creek or Allen Bill Pond carparks. The trail pops in and out of the dense forest, while running parallel to Iron Creek for most of its length. To access Elbow Trail, follow Sundog Loop out from West Bragg Creek or access it directly via the Allen Bill Pond Day Use Area.

## TRAILHEAD | N50 56.292 W114 41.460 (NORTH); N50 54.096 W114 41.228 (SOUTH)

From West Bragg Creek access Elbow Trail via Sundog Loop or directly access the southern trailhead from the Allen Bill Pond parking area. Allen Bill Pond is located on Hwy 66, west of Bragg Creek.

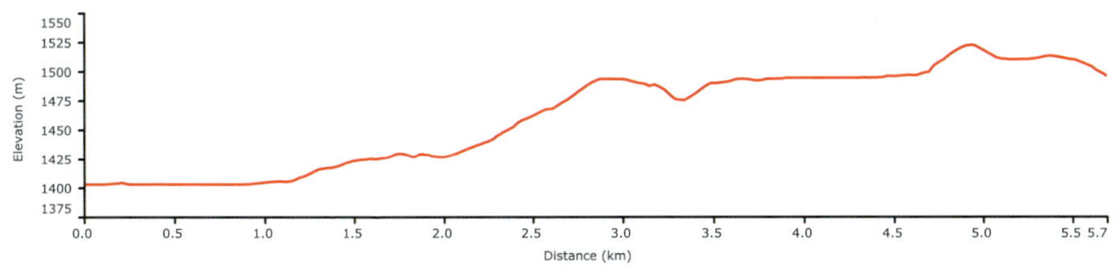

# 41 | IRON SPRINGS | 💀 💀

| | |
|---|---|
| Distance: 4.6 km | Technical Rating: Beginner |
| Time: 30 min - 1 hr | Physical Rating: Easy |
| Elevation Gain: 104 m | Season: June - October |
| Elevation Loss: 149 m | Trail Type: X-Country |

Iron Springs is a popular x-country ski trail in the winter and a heavily-used equestrian trail in the summer. Mountain biking is allowed, but not a whole lot of fun in the spring or after heavy rain due to the many mud bogs and high horse traffic. It is a scenic trail with minimal elevation gains and very few gradual climbs.

Iron Springs is a wide doubletrack that pops in and out of the woods, offering many scenic viewpoints along the way. Best used to access Boundary Ridge and/or Snagmore in the West Bragg Creek Trails network, Iron Springs serves as a great connecting route. If you prefer riding doubletrack over the flowy intermediate singletrack trails in the area, then this one is for you. Families looking for something tame may loop Iron Springs with Elbow Trail for an 11 km beginner loop starting at the West Bragg Creek parking area.

## TRAILHEAD | N50 56.304 W114 41.151

Access Iron Springs directly via Sundog Loop from the West Bragg Creek parking lot. From Bragg Creek take Balsam Ave. west to Centre Ave. Turn southwest (left) at the T-junction onto Centre Ave. Drive southwest on Centre Ave, which will turn into Township Rd. 232. Continue on Township Rd. 232 until you hit the gravel road. Cross the cattle guard and drive to the well-marked parking area 500 m ahead on your right. The trail is accessed via Sundog Loop south of the parking lot.

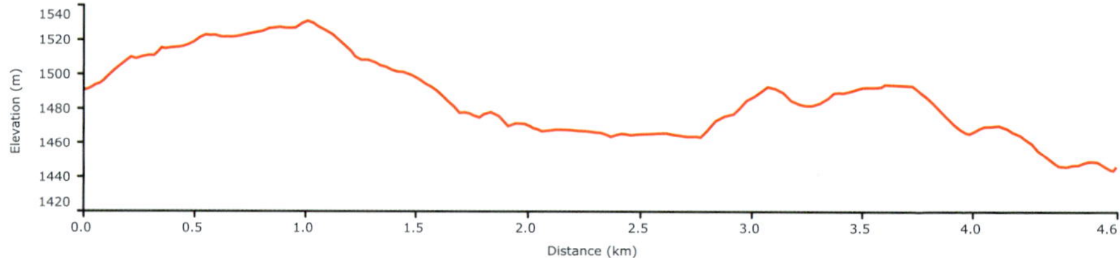

# 42 | BOUNDARY RIDGE | 💀 💀 💀

| | |
|---|---|
| Distance: 5.3 km | Technical Rating: Intermediate |
| Time: 45 min – 1.5 hrs | Physical Rating: Moderate |
| Elevation Gain: 157 m | Season: June - October |
| Elevation Loss: 199 m | Trail Type: X-Country |

Boundary Ridge is a sweet intermediate singletrack trail located in the West Bragg Creek Trails network. The trail may be ridden in either direction, as an out-and-back or as a part of a larger loop. If you're looking for a loop to ride in the area that includes Boundary Ridge, consider Goldilocks or Southern Flow.

Boundary Ridge best flows south to north, although it may be ridden either direction and as an out-and-back. The trail runs through the woods, popping out at various points to offer some great views of the surrounding hillside meadows. The rider will be treated to some fun switchback climbs and speedy descents on this pristine singletrack trail. Built to utilize the surrounding terrain, Boundary Ridge rolls really nicely up and down. This is a great trail for beginners who would like to progress their riding, and a fun ride for intermediate to advanced riders. The word that best describes the singletrack trails in West Bragg Creek is FLOW; Boundary Ridge epitomizes this description.

### TRAILHEAD | N50 56.895 W114 41.606 (WEST BRAGG); N50 55.300 W114 40.465 (SOUTH)

From Bragg Creek take Balsam Ave. west to Centre Ave. Turn southwest (left) at the T-junction onto Centre Ave. Drive southwest on Centre Ave., which will turn into Township Rd. 232. Continue on Township Rd. 232 until you hit the gravel road. Cross the cattle guard and drive to the well-marked parking area 500 m ahead on your right. The trail begins south of the parking lot.

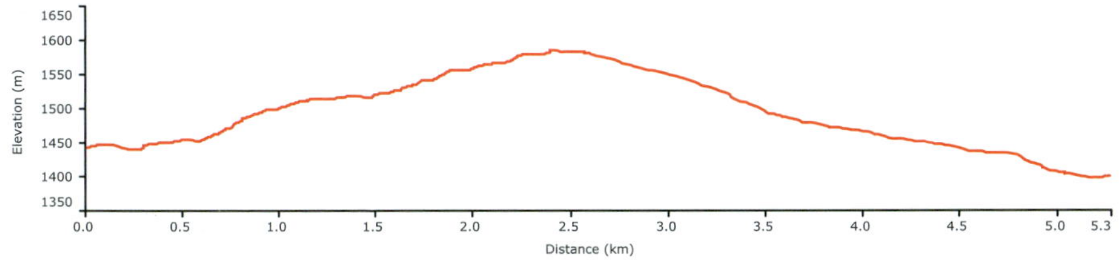

# 43 | BRAGGIN RIGHTS | 💀 💀 💀 💀

| | |
|---|---|
| Distance: 3.6 km | Technical Rating: Intermediate |
| Time: 25 min - 1 hr | Physical Rating: Moderate |
| Elevation Gain: 130 m | Season: June - October |
| Elevation Loss: 33 m | Trail Type: X-Country |

Braggin Rights is an intermediate singletrack trail located in West Bragg Creek. It begins with a gradual climb, heading north from the day use and parking area. This is not a very long trail, but when combined with others in the area you're sure to get a great workout. The trail is a lot of fun to climb and makes for a fast and exciting descent. The climb combines a few short and steep sections right at the beginning of the trail, followed by a steady, low grade, switchback climb up to the top of the trail. Alternatively, coming down Braggin Rights provides its own kind of excitement. The short steep ups now become sections of trail that allow you to pick up speed and gain some air when riding fast or just act as a nice roller coaster effect. The trail flows really nicely either direction, so ride it both ways to figure out your maximum flow. Watch out for other users when coming down the trail as this is the main connector to Long Distance and may get busy during the weekends.

## TRAILHEAD | N50 56.911 W114 41.616

From Bragg Creek take Balsam Ave. west to Centre Ave. Turn southwest (left) at the T-junction onto Centre Ave. Drive southwest on Centre Ave., which will turn into Township Rd. 232. Continue on Township Rd. 232 until you hit the gravel road. Cross the cattle guard and drive to the well-marked parking area 500 m ahead on your right. The trail begins at the north end of the parking lot.

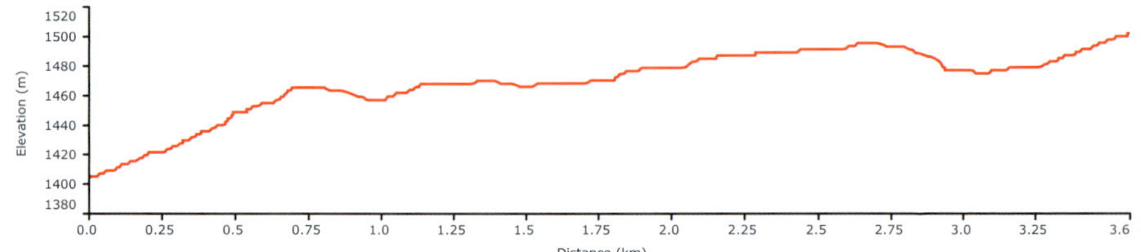

# 44 | GOLDILOCKS LOOP | 

| | |
|---|---|
| Distance: 9.2 km | Technical Rating: Intermediate |
| Time: 1 – 2 hrs | Physical Rating: Moderate |
| Elevation Gain: 340 m | Season: June - October |
| Elevation Loss: 342 m | Trail Type: X-Country |

Goldilocks Loop is located in the West Bragg Creek Trails network, combining two fun singletrack trails to form a shorter loop one can mountain bike after work or when short on time. Begin your ride up (south) Ranger Summit. Climb until you reach the clearly marked Strange Brew trailhead, about 4.3 km up Ranger Summit. From there take Strange Brew (east) back down to Boundary Ridge junction. At the Boundary Ridge junction, turn left (north) and pedal the remaining 1 km back to the West Bragg Creek carpark.

Goldilocks Loop starts with a switchbacking singletrack climb up Ranger Summit through a heavily forested area. The long climb is gradual, making it a real cardio workout while still remaining fun. The descent down is taken via Strange Brew, a fast-paced affair when you let yourself open it up. The Loop ends with a short section on Boundary Ridge, descending the remainder of the way to the carpark.

## TRAILHEAD | N50 56.898 W114 41.584

From Bragg Creek take Balsam Ave. west to Centre Ave. Turn southwest (left) at the T-junction onto Centre Ave. Drive southwest on Centre Ave., which will turn into Township Rd. 232. Continue on Township Rd. 232 until you hit the gravel road. Cross the cattle guard and drive to the well-marked parking area 500 m ahead on your right. Begin Goldilocks by riding south on Ranger Summit directly from the carpark.

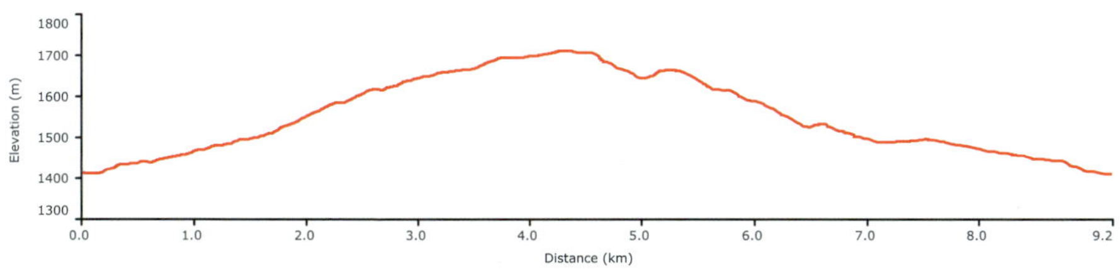

# 45 | LONG DISTANCE | 💀💀💀💀

| | |
|---|---|
| Distance: 8.5 km | Technical Rating: Intermediate |
| Time: 1 – 2 hrs | Physical Rating: Moderate - Hard |
| Elevation Gain: 248 m | Season: June - October |
| Elevation Loss: 286 m | Trail Type: X-Country |

Long Distance is an awesome singletrack trail located in the West Bragg Creek Trails network that winds and switchbacks its way up to connect with Telephone Loop. It may be ridden as an out-and-back, or combined with either Telephone Loop or Braggin Rights for a fabulous loop.

When starting from the West Bragg parking area, ride north on Braggin Rights to connect with Long Distance 600 m up the trail. From the trailhead Long Distance begins to climb up a few steep inclines, switchbacking for the first part of the climb. The switchbacks provide short sections of gradual grade allowing the rider a chance to catch their breath. After about 2 km of climbing the trail grade levels out for a short while. The terrain varies along Long Distance, keeping the ride interesting. The rider will encounter long wooded sections along with breaks in the forest offering up some incredible views. At the 2.9 km juncture, the trail meets up with Reconnect and Demi-Tel, providing an option to loop back to the parking lot. Continue on up to the end of Long Distance and connect with Telephone Loop (ride east/right) to head back towards the parking area. I recommend doubling back along Long Distance for a fun and exciting descent back to Braggin Rights and eventually the carpark.

### TRAILHEAD | N50 56.898 W114 41.584 (PARKING); N50 56.948 W114 42.162 (TH)

From Bragg Creek take Balsam Ave. west to Centre Ave. Turn southwest (left) at the T-junction onto Centre Ave. Drive southwest on Centre Ave., which will turn into Township Rd. 232. Continue on Township Rd. 232 until you hit the gravel road. Cross the cattle guard and drive to the well-marked parking area 500 m ahead on your right. Long Distance is accessed via Braggin Rights, 600 m north from the carpark.

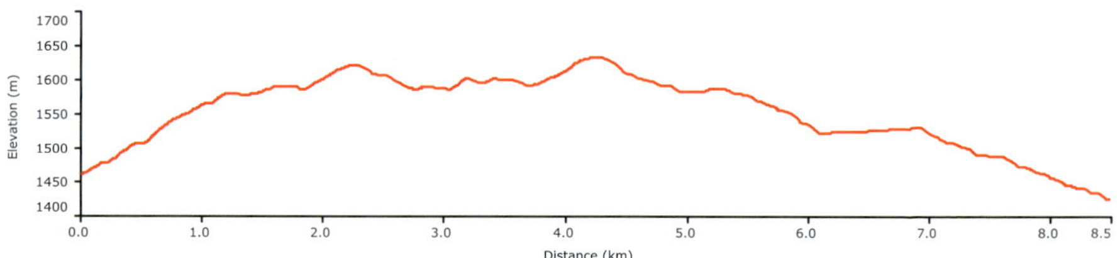

Braggin Rights

# 46 | NORTHERN FLOW LOOP | 💀💀💀💀

**Distance: 8.6 km**
**Time: 45 min – 1.5 hrs**
**Elevation Gain: 272 m**
**Elevation Loss: 273 m**

**Technical Rating: Intermediate**
**Physical Rating: Moderate**
**Season: June - October**
**Trail Type: X-Country**

Northern Flow Loop combines some of the best singletrack trails located on the north side of the West Bragg Creek Trails network to form a short but fun loop. The loop may be ridden in either direction, but I found it to flow best when ridden clockwise. Begin the loop directly from the West Bragg Creek carpark by riding north on Braggin Rights. Mountain bike up Braggin Rights to Reconnect and over to Long Distance. From Long Distance head south (right) back down to the carpark. This loop has minimal elevation gain and can be ridden in 45 minutes or less when cranking it, or in about an hour and a half at cruising speed. This is a great loop to do if you're short on time and want to combine a few of the really fun trails located in the area.

## TRAILHEAD | N50 56.898 W114 41.584

From Bragg Creek take Balsam Ave. west to Centre Ave. Turn southwest (left) at the T-junction on to Centre Ave. Drive southwest on Centre Ave., which will turn into Township Rd. 232. Continue on Township Rd. 232 until you hit the gravel road. Cross the cattle guard and drive to the well-marked parking area 500 m ahead on your right. The loop begins north of the parking lot up Braggin Rights.

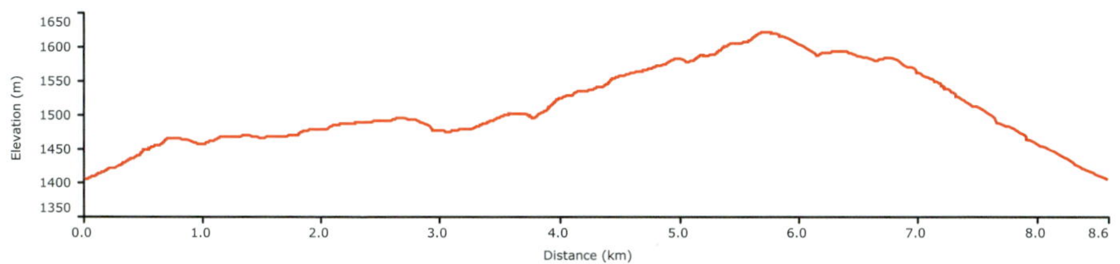

# 47 | RANGER SUMMIT | 💀💀💀💀💀

| | |
|---|---|
| Distance: 4.8 km | Technical Rating: Intermediate |
| Time: 1 - 2 hrs | Physical Rating: Moderate |
| Elevation Gain: 308 m | Season: June - October |
| Elevation Loss: 43 m | Trail Type: X-Country |

Ranger Summit is one of the recently built multi-use singletrack trails located in West Bragg Creek Trails network. This trail is a "must do" ride when visiting the area. It begins south of the West Bragg Creek carpark, across the West Bragg bridge, switchbacking up Ranger Ridge. Halfway up Ranger Summit is the turn-off for Strange Brew. For those looking for a quick singletrack loop that takes about an hour to complete, take the turn-off; otherwise, continue on up Ranger Summit. Once you've reached the actual Summit, the trail begins to descend southeast. Turn around at this point if you're riding Ranger Summit as an out-and-back, or continue on down to the Elbow Trail and the Snagmore junction. About 300 m down the descent the trail gets a bit more technical. At this point you're no longer on Ranger Summit, but rather on Sugar Mama. Sugar Mama is an unsanctioned trail - ride this trail at your own risk as it is not officially maintained. Once you hit Elbow Trail, to complete your loop, take Snagmore to Boundary Ridge, finishing at the West Bragg carpark.

Ranger Summit trail was built for the intermediate rider. Beginners with a little experience will also enjoy this fun ride up and great descent down. It may be ridden as an out-and-back, or as a part of the Goldilocks or Southern Flow Loops.

### TRAILHEAD | N50 56.886 W114 41.604

From Bragg Creek take Balsam Ave. west to Centre Ave. Turn southwest (left) at the T-junction on to Centre Ave. Drive southwest on Centre Ave., which will turn into Township Rd. 232. Continue on Township Rd. 232 until you hit the gravel road. Cross the cattle guard and drive to the well-marked parking area 500 m ahead on your right. Ranger Summit starts south of the parking lot.

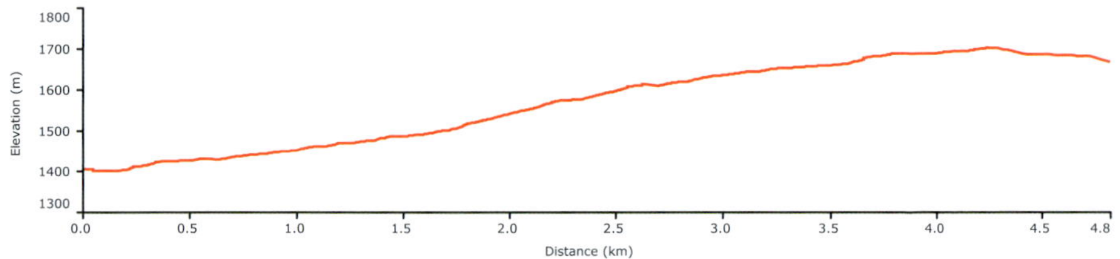

# 48 | RECONNECT | 💀 💀 💀

| | |
|---|---|
| Distance: 1.6 km | Technical Rating: Intermediate |
| Time: 10 - 30 min | Physical Rating: Moderate |
| Elevation Gain: 98 m | Season: June - October |
| Elevation Loss: 11 m | Trail Type: X-Country |

Reconnect is a short but fun connector trail located in the West Bragg Creek Trails network. It may be ridden either direction, flowing really nicely both ways. Riding it east to west is much quicker, with more descending to be had. When riding Reconnect from the west side, the singletrack trail runs through the woods crossing a wooden bridge built over a creek and popping out onto Telephone Loop. Continuing across Telephone Loop, the trail climbs out of the trees, and up the long and narrow switchback, taking the rider over to the Long Distance trail junction. The purpose of Reconnect, as the name suggests, is to connect the rider with Long Distance or Telephone Loop when riding Braggin Rights north.

**TRAILHEAD | N50 57.536 W114 43.531 (WEST TH); N50 57.623 W114 42.964 (EAST TH)**

From Bragg Creek take Balsam Ave. west to Centre Ave. Turn southwest (left) at the T-junction on to Centre Ave. Drive southwest on Centre Ave., which will turn into Township Rd. 232. Continue on Township Rd. 232 until you hit the gravel road. Cross the cattle guard and drive to the well-marked parking area 500 m ahead on your right. From the parking lot access Reconnect via Braggin Rights or Long Distance.

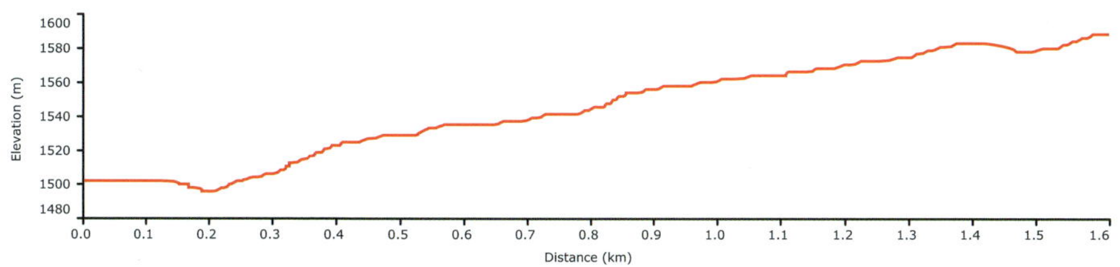

# 49 | SNAGMORE | 💀💀💀💀

|  |  |
|---|---|
| Distance: 5.2 km | Technical Rating: Intermediate |
| Time: 30 min – 1.5 hrs | Physical Rating: Moderate |
| Elevation Gain: 186 m | Season: June - October |
| Elevation Loss: 140 m | Trail Type: X-Country |

Snagmore is a multi-use singletrack trail that may be ridden either direction. For the best flow, ride it south to north, accessing it via Elbow Trail. The trail offers some amazing views along a number of viewpoints, while covering some great rolling terrain. Similar to the fun singletrack trails built in the area, Snagmore is one of the more diverse trails and one of my favourites to ride. When you're not climbing up gradual switchbacks and along various ridge lines, you'll be descending some smooth and flowy singletrack along sections of well-built bench cut trail. Overall, the trail is super smooth and fun to ride; there are no huge technical sections here, except for a few tech moves when climbing or descending at high speeds.

Snagmore is very well marked, as are other newly built singletrack trails in the area. All major junctions include an overview map showing your location. Please give right of way to equestrians and hikers found using these trails on busy weekends.

**TRAILHEAD | N50 54.481 W114 40.743 (SOUTH); N50 55.432 W114 40.476 (NORTH)**

From Bragg Creek take Balsam Ave. west to Centre Ave. Turn southwest (left) at the T-junction onto Centre Ave. Drive southwest on Centre Ave., which will turn into Township Rd. 232. Continue on Township Rd. 232 until you hit the gravel road. Cross the cattle guard and drive to the well-marked parking area 500 m ahead on your right. From there access Snagmore via Elbow Trail, Iron Springs or Boundary Ridge.

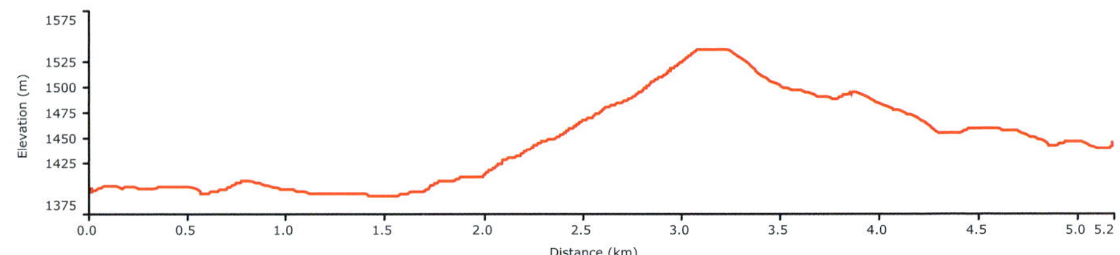

# 50 | SOUTHERN FLOW | 

Distance: 18.2 km
Time: 2 - 3 hrs
Elevation Gain: 647 m
Elevation Loss: 651 m

Technical Rating: Intermediate
Physical Rating: Hard
Season: June - October
Trail Type: X-Country

Southern Flow Loop is located in the West Bragg Creek Trails network, and combines some of the area's best singletrack trails into one large loop that will take most riders between two to three hours to complete. This loop offers everything a rider could hope for: long, steady climbs to some incredible viewpoints, along with fast, flowy and technical descents. The loop is best ridden counter clockwise for maximum flow, but may be ridden in either direction if you're up for a challenge.

To begin Southern Flow, pedal across the Bragg Creek bridge from the West Bragg parking area. Ride up Ranger Summit trail, climbing to the summit. Take a break at the summit to recover from the lung and leg burn before beginning to descend about 350 m to the trail junction on your left. Follow this trail (Sugar Mama, an unofficial trail which riders should ride at their own risk) down a thrilling and fast descent to link up with Snagmore, once you pop out on Elbow Trail – Snagmore trailhead is located straight ahead, across Elbow Trail. Ride along Snagmore's undulating singletrack, crossing Elbow Trail and Iron Springs in several sections along the way. Once you hit Boundary Ridge, you will climb for another 2 km before you begin your last fun and flowy descent back to the start of the loop. Watch out for oncoming traffic and give right of way to hikers and equestrians when out riding in this area.

## TRAILHEAD | N50 56.898 W114 41.584 (PARKING)

From Bragg Creek take Balsam Ave. west to Centre Ave. Turn southwest (left) at the T-junction onto Centre Ave. Drive southwest on Centre Ave., which will turn into Township Rd. 232. Continue on Township Rd. 232 until you hit the gravel road. Cross the cattle guard and drive to the well-marked parking area 500 m ahead on your right. Start Southern Flow by riding south on Ranger Summit accessed via the carpark.

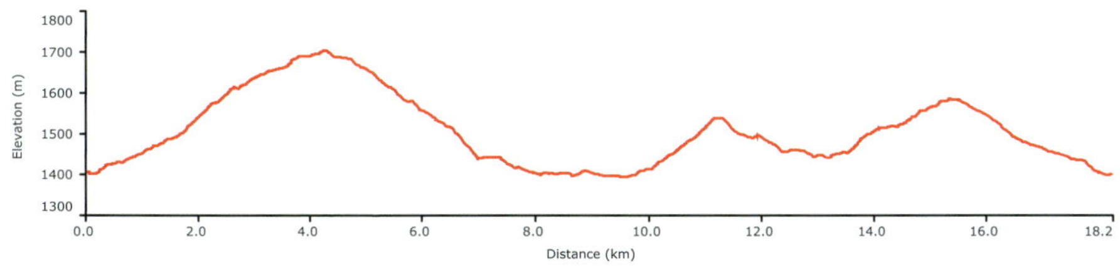

# 51 | STRANGE BREW | 💀💀💀

| | |
|---|---|
| Distance: 3.3 km | Technical Rating: Intermediate |
| Time: 20 – 45 min | Physical Rating: Easy |
| Elevation Gain: 39 m | Season: June - October |
| Elevation Loss: 253 m | Trail Type: X-Country |

Strange Brew is a part of the West Bragg Creek Trails network. It is a multi-use singletrack trail that may be ridden either direction, but for maximum flow, access it via Ranger Summit and ride it east. It is a reclaimed trail recently upgraded by the trail builders to the same sustainable standards as the newly built singletrack trails in the area. Short reroutes and tread construction have been done to maximize the flow of this trail. Strange Brew is a good option if you're looking to ride a shorter loop, combining Ranger Summit with Strange Brew for a 1 – 1.5 hour ride; this is dubbed the Goldilocks Loop.

Strange Brew offers a fun and fast descent down from Ranger Summit. It's all singletrack, with a few short technical sections. A great viewpoint at Barruch's Corner is located near the beginning of the western part of this trail and makes for a nice rest stop. Following the viewpoint, the trail begins to descend down the flowy singletrack, switchbacking in a few sections, before connecting directly with Boundary Ridge. From there ride Boundary Ridge trail north (left) back to the West Bragg parking lot.

*Important note:* Strange Brew should not be ridden when wet in order to prevent tread damage until after August 2013, once the trail has had a chance to settle. Please respect this request from the trail builders and volunteers to keep the trail from severe damage.

## TRAILHEAD | N50 55.477 W114 42.310 (WEST TH); N50 56.345 W114 41.056 (EAST TH)

From Bragg Creek take Balsam Ave. west to Centre Ave. Turn southwest (left) at the T-junction onto Centre Ave. Drive southwest on Centre Ave., which will turn into Township Rd. 232. Continue on Township Rd. 232 until you hit the gravel road. Cross the cattle guard and drive to the well-marked parking area 500 m ahead on your right. From there access Strange Brew via Ranger Summit or Boundary Ridge.

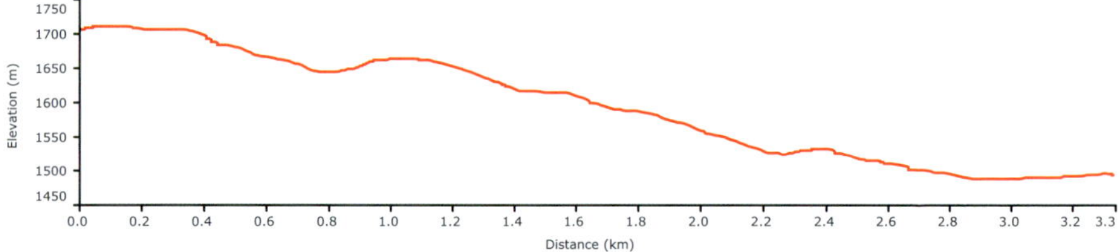

# 52 | TELEPHONE LOOP | 

**Distance:** 12.6 km
**Time:** 1.5 - 3 hrs
**Elevation Gain:** 337 m
**Elevation Loss:** 303 m

**Technical Rating:** Intermediate
**Physical Rating:** Moderate
**Season:** June - October
**Trail Type:** X-Country

The 5.9 km leg of Telephone Loop located on the east side of the West Bragg Creek Trails network is only partially maintained for summer use. The remaining 6.6 km on the west side is not recommended for summer use as it is only maintained during the winter months for skiing. The trail is made up of narrow doubletrack, with a few short sections of singletrack scattered throughout. A popular trail amongst equestrians, it is not recommended for riding when wet. Spring is a particularly bad time to get on this trail as it takes a while to dry out and will be considerably muddy. Provided that sufficient funding is donated and government approval secured, the east side of Telephone Loop may be upgraded in 2013. To donate, please visit http://braggcreektrails.org

There is not a lot of elevation gain on this trail, but it does contain a number of short steep ups and quick downs as it rolls along the undulating terrain. Braggin Rights, Disconnect (under construction), Reconnect and Long Distance are the new singletrack trails that either cross or connect to Telephone Loop. With so many new singletrack trails built in the area, there is no need to waste your time on this ride, unless you're connecting it with one of the newly built trails to form a loop.

## TRAILHEAD | N50 56.925 W114 41.569

From Bragg Creek take Balsam Ave. west to Centre Ave. Turn southwest (left) at the T-junction onto Centre Ave. Drive southwest on Centre Ave., which will turn into Township Rd. 232. Continue on Township Rd. 232 until you hit the gravel road. Cross the cattle guard and drive to the well-marked parking area 500 m ahead on your right. Access Telephone loop directly from the parking lot. The summer trailhead is located on the northeast end of the parking lot.

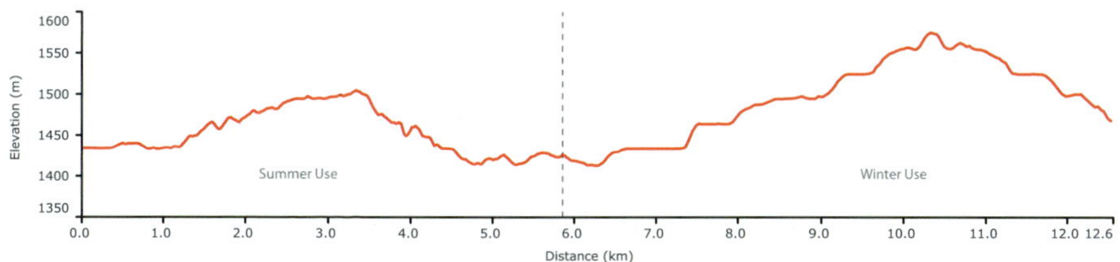

Jumpingpound Ridge

MAP 6: SIBBALD AREA
N
Scenic Lookout
Kananaskis River
40
Lusk Creek Day Use
68
Lusk Pass
Mount Baldy
Baldy Pass
Eagle Hill Trail
Deer Ridge
Ole Buck Loop
Ole Buck Mountain
68
Sibbald Lake Rec. Area
Demonstration Forest Loop
Jumpingpound Loop
1372
Spruce Woods Day Use
May 1a south of Dawson
Dawson Recreational Area
Powderface trail closed Dec. 1 – May 1a south of Dawson
Cox Hill
Tom Snow
Pinetop Hill
Jumpingpound Ridge
Jumpingpound Summit
Jumpingpound Mountain
Moose Mountain Trail
Moose Mountain
2 km
TransCanada Highway 1
Paved Road/Highway
Dirt Road
Trailhead
Water
Height in metres (m)
Trail Junction
Beginner Trails
Intermediate Trails
Advanced / Expert Trails
Camping
Toilets / Outhouse
Parking

Jumpingpound Ridge

# SIBBALD AREA

The Sibbald Area is located 50 km west of Calgary. It is accessed via Hwy 68 or Powderface Trail. Hwy 68 is a gravel road between Hwy 40 and the Powderface Trail Road, but is paved between Hwy 1 and Pinetop Recreation area (the east end of the Jumpingpound Loop). Powderface Trail is all gravel and narrow in sections, take care when driving these backcountry access routes. Please also note that Powderface Trail is closed to vehicles December 1 to May 14.

The trails found in the Sibbald area consist of some big alpine rides, along with a few shorter routes suitable for families and accessible from the Sibbald Lake Recreational Area. Most of the trails are remote in nature and as such it is advised that you don't ride alone or at least inform someone you know as to where you're heading. Bring bear spray and during the busy summer months watch out for other trail users.

The majority of the trails found in the Sibbald area typically take at least until the end of June to dry out. In some cases you'll still find snow on the higher elevation rides up until the middle of July. Jumpingpound Loop is a nice intermediate lower elevation singletrack ride that can thaw out as early as the end of May, depending on the amount of snow received the winter before. The Loop is worth checking out if you're itching to ride. The "must do" ride in the area is none other than Jumpingpound Ridge to Cox Hill, offering up some incredible alpine riding. An epic x-country ride with incredible 360 degree views of the surrounding mountains, Jumpingpound Ridge to Cox Hill will not disappoint.

# 53 | DEER RIDGE TRAIL | 💀

| | |
|---|---|
| Distance: 3.5 km | Technical Rating: Beginner |
| Time: 20 min - 1 hr | Physical Rating: Moderate |
| Elevation Gain: 213 m | Season: June - October |
| Elevation Loss: 196 m | Trail Type: X-Country |

Deer Ridge Trail is a multi-use singletrack accessed via the Sibbald Lake Recreation Area. The trail gets very overgrown in the summer and is not the best option for a mountain bike ride; look to Eagle Hill or better yet Ole Buck Loop for a family-friendly riding experience if you're camping in the area and looking to mountain bike. Deer Ridge winds its way around a swamp and can be very wet and boggy during the spring. Route finding around this track can be treacherous as the trail does not receive much attention. Riders will spend a large section of this trail walking, weaving their way through the swampy and mud boggy sections. There is no real reward for slugging it out on this trail. It may be best to leave this one for equestrians to explore, as this trail is probably better on a horse.

Deer Ridge Trail may be combined with Eagle Hill Trail to create a loop of about 6.5 km in length; if you still wish to explore this ride. Bring a compass and map or GPS device as route finding on the overgrown trail is a challenge.

## TRAILHEAD | N51 02.673 W114 52.136

From Hwy 1, take Hwy 68 south to Sibbald Lake Recreation Area. Park by the day use area bathrooms and look for the Eagle Hill and Deer Ridge trailheads southwest of the parking lot. The trailhead is well marked. Head west on Eagle Hill Trail for about 300 m to the trailhead for Deer Ridge Trail; it is not marked. Look for a wooden bridge crossing a creek, to your left, to start Deer Ridge Trail.

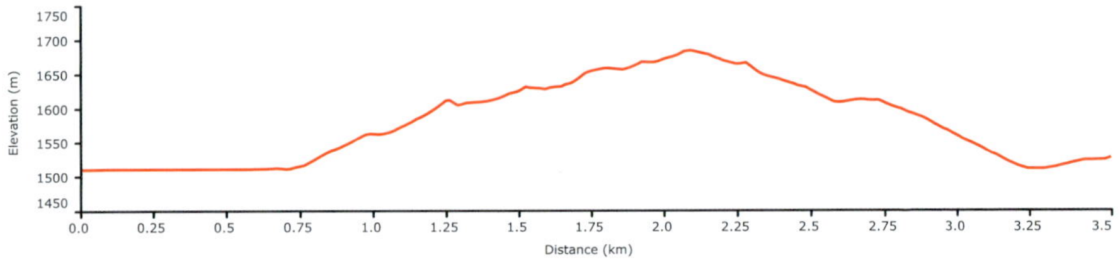

# 54 | JUMPINGPOUND LOOP | 

| | |
|---|---|
| Distance: 9.4 km | Technical Rating: Beginner - Intermediate |
| Time: 45 min - 1.5 hrs | Physical Rating: Easy |
| Elevation Gain: 248 m | Season: May - October |
| Elevation Loss: 242 m | Trail Type: X-Country |

Jumpingpound Loop is a super sweet and fast singletrack ride suitable for all levels of riders. This trail has a very moderate gradient with little elevation gain – not very common for Kananaskis Country. It may be ridden clockwise or counter-clockwise; the choice is yours.

The fast and flowy singletrack can be taken at speed for the more advanced rider, while beginners will appreciate the little elevation gain and the rolling nature of this track. There are a number of river/creek crossings over wooden manmade bridges. Some great views of Jumpingpound Creek can be found on the south side of the track. Enjoy this ride in the early spring, as it's one of the first to thaw out in the Sibbald Area.

**TRAILHEAD | N51 02.627 W114 46.654 (PINE GROVE); N51 02.203 W114 43.769 (PINETOP)**

Take the TransCanada Hwy 1 to Sibbald Creek Trail (Hwy 68) and head south. Park at the Pinetop Picnic Area and start the trail from there – either direction, you choose. You can also drive to the Pine Grove Group Camping Area and start from there.

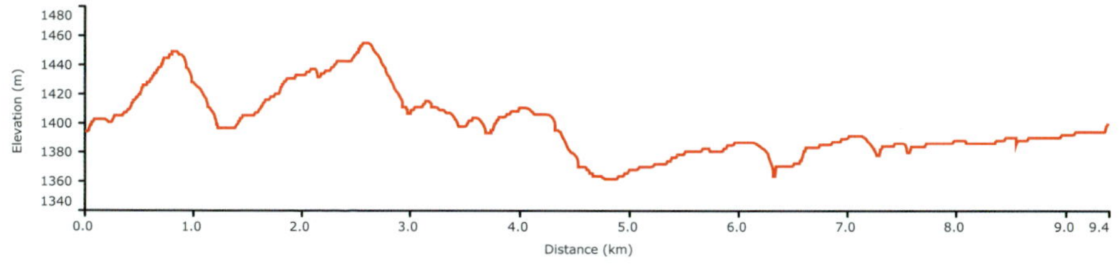

# 55 | EAGLE HILL TRAIL | 

Distance: 7.2 km (one way)

Time: 1 – 2 hrs

Elevation Gain: 343 m

Elevation Loss: 106 m

Technical Rating: Intermediate

Physical Rating: Moderate

Season: June - October

Trail Type: X-Country

Eagle Hill Trail is a scenic ride through foothills, providing great views of the Bow River Valley. The trail combines singletrack with doubletrack, which can be overgrown in a number of sections throughout the summer. Although the trail is maintained for summer use, I found loads of deadfall to be present at certain times of the year. Ride with care and stay on your toes when descending so you don't run into one of the fallen trees. Eagle Hill may be ridden as an out-and-back, or as a lolly pop loop when combining it with Deer Ridge Trail. I would recommend skipping Deer Ridge altogether and ride this one on its own.

At one point in time Eagle Hill Trail extended all the way from Dawson Recreation Area to Sibbald Lake Recreation Area. The section between Dawson and Sibbald is now almost all overgrown, hard to follow, and broken up by newly built log roads. It's best to avoid this 4 km section altogether. From Sibbald Lake Recreation Area the trail is still intact and takes you to a scenic lookout point worth checking out if you're camping in the area.

## TRAILHEAD | N51 02.763 W114 52.045

From Hwy 1, take Hwy 68 south to Sibbald Lake Recreation Area. Park by the day use area bathrooms and look for the Eagle Hill trailhead southwest of the parking lot. The trailhead is well marked and heads west along the hillside.

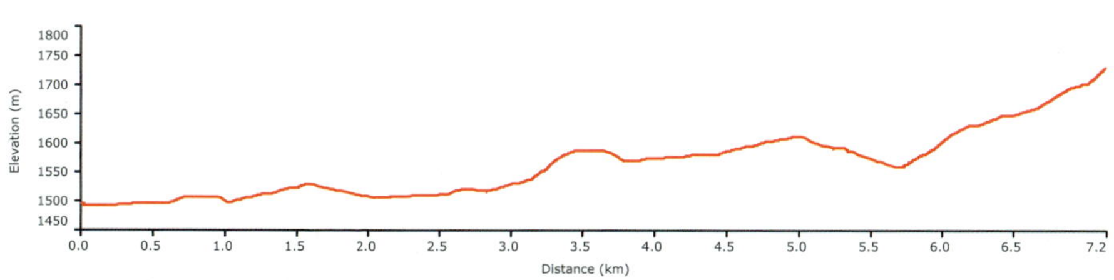

# 56 | LUSK PASS | 💀💀

| | |
|---|---|
| Distance: 8.0 km (one way) | Technical Rating: Intermediate |
| Time: 1 - 2 hrs | Physical Rating: Moderate - Hard |
| Elevation Gain: 365 m | Season: June - October |
| Elevation Loss: 125 m | Trail Type: X-Country |

Lusk Pass may be ridden out-and-back or used to access Jumpingpound Ridge. It may also be combined with Baldy Pass Trail to form a short 5.5 km loop. The trail is mostly doubletrack and not worth the effort on its own. There are plenty of other options in the area if you're looking for a trail with sweet singletrack and great views taking you high up into the alpine, including Jumpingpound Ridge to Cox Hill.

The start of Lusk Pass is found on the south side of Hwy 68 across from the Lusk Creek Recreation Area. Look for the trail running up the embankment across the highway. Once up the embankment you will approach the first junction, 200 m from Hwy 68. At the junction turn left onto the narrow singletrack that runs along a ravine and heads into the woods just ahead. From here on the trail is easy to follow. Lusk Pass will begin to gradually climb up a sandy and loose doubletrack which has seen better days; parts of the trail are very much eroded. After about the 1.5 km mark the trail gets better. It becomes hard packed and easier to pedal as it continues on up to the false summit. The last few climbs to the false summit get considerably steeper, providing a real challenge for fit and experienced riders. However, don't expect many views once you reach the top due to the low elevation and thick forest. From there the ride down to Powderface Trail, a dirt road, and the Jumpingpoung Ridge trailhead is fast and fun. Enjoy the descent – after all, you've earned it!

## TRAILHEAD | N51 01.960 W115 00.811 (LUSK CREEK); N51 01.920 W115 00.827 (TH)

Take Hwy 40 south to Hwy 68, a dirt road. Turn on to Hwy 68 and continue east for about 1 km to the Lusk Creek Recreation Area. The trail starts from across Hwy 68, up the embankment. There are no trailhead markings, but the trail is easy to spot and is located to your left about 200 m up from Hwy 68.

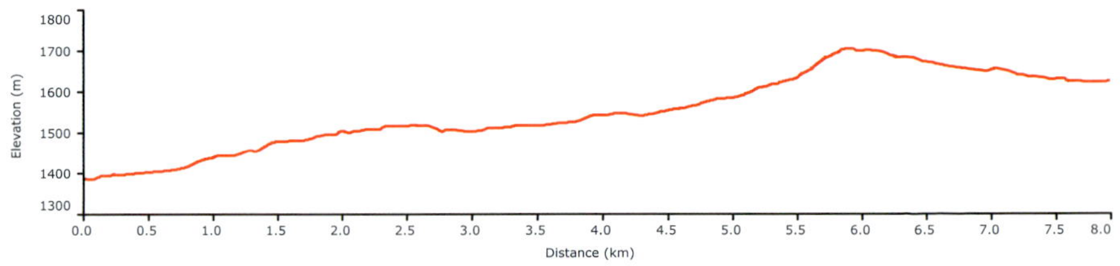

# 57 | OLE BUCK LOOP | 💀 💀

Distance: 4.7 km
Time: 30 min - 1 hr
Elevation Gain: 177 m
Elevation Loss: 170 m

Technical Rating: Intermediate
Physical Rating: Moderate
Season: June - October
Trail Type: X-Country

Ole Buck Loop is best ridden clockwise for added flow, but can be ridden either direction. The trail is a short singletrack loop with two lookout points, the first of which offers the best view on the trail. When riding the trail clockwise, once you come to the first lookout (marked by a wooden bench), keep left following the hiker sign on the tree; going straight leads to a dead end.

The ride is 100% flowy singletrack for the first 3/4 of trail. The last section can be overgrown in the summer as it runs through a field. Ole Buck Loop is a fun ride to enjoy with your family when camping or visiting the area, but not worth a special trip out. On a hot day bring your swim suit and jump in Sibbald Lake to cool off and enjoy the water after your ride.

## TRAILHEAD | N51 02.855 W114 51.960

Take Hwy 68 to Sibbald Lake Recreational Area. Drive to the picnic area, straight ahead, and look for the well-marked trailhead with map showing the direction of Ole Buck Loop.

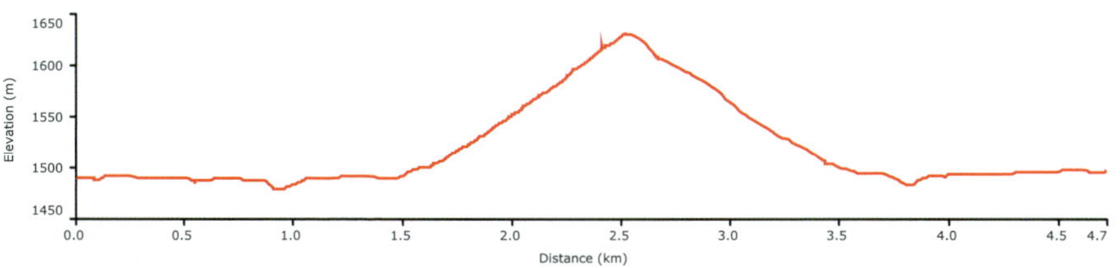

# 58 | COX HILL TRAIL | 💀 💀 💀 💀

**Distance:** 9.4 km (one way)
**Time:** 2 - 4 hrs
**Elevation Gain:** 857 m
**Elevation Loss:** 284 m

**Technical Rating:** Advanced
**Physical Rating:** Extreme
**Season:** June - October
**Trail Type:** X-Country

Cox Hill is a classic big alpine ride located in the Sibbald area. It is best combined with Jumpingpound Ridge for a very rewarding big mountain ride. However, it may also be ridden on its own as an out-and-back. The trail starts from the Dawson Recreation Area. The trailhead is located on the east side of the parking lot and is well marked. Follow it out, across the beautifully constructed pedestrian bridge, up the short hill to the T-intersection. At the intersection take a right (south), and begin your ride up the steady and very long climb. The trail continues to climb for about 6 km until it reaches a grassy hilltop with incredibly stunning panoramic views of the surrounding mountains. From here, turn around if you're tired and looking to shorten your ride. Otherwise, continue on down a 2 km descent to the final 1 km climb up to the Jumpingpound Ridge intersection. At the intersection head left and out onto Jumpingpound Ridge to have a look around. You may also choose to take Jumpingpound Ridge west (right) down to the Powderface Trail and ride back along the dirt road to Dawson Recreation Area. My suggestion would be to head back the way you came, ending your ride down the fast and exciting 6 km singletrack descent. This is a great reward for the slug up.

For more information on how to best combine Cox Hill for one incredible ride, consider the Jumpingpound Ridge to Cox Hill combo described on page 115, one of my favourite x-country rides in Kananaskis Country.

## TRAILHEAD | N51 01.387 W114 52.916

Take Hwy 68 to Powderface Trail. Turn south on Powderface Trail and drive to the Dawson Recreational Area, located about 3 km south of Hwy 68.

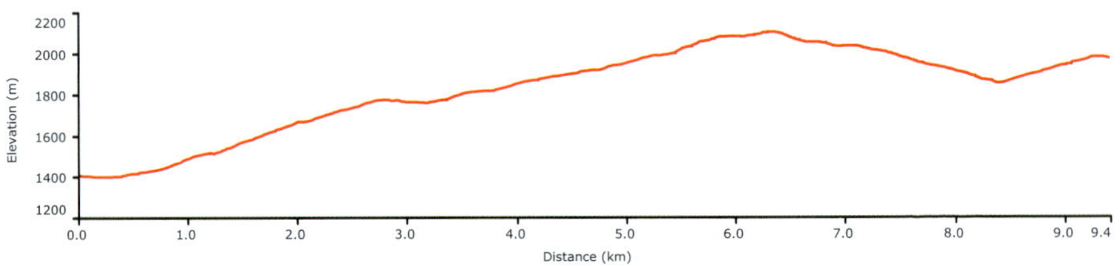

# 59 | JUMPINGPOUND RIDGE TRAIL | 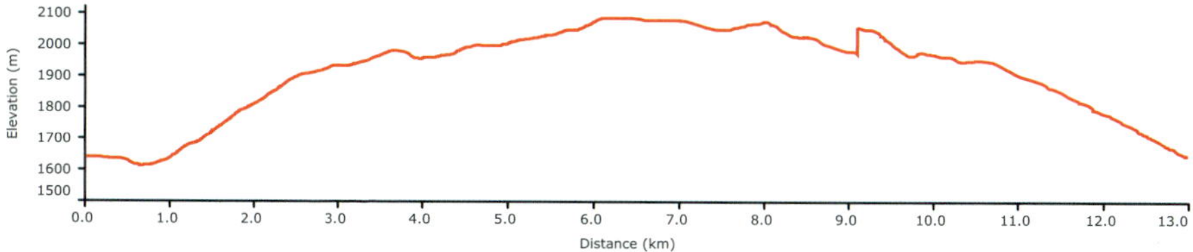

**Distance:** 13 km (one way)  
**Time:** 2 - 4 hrs  
**Elevation Gain:** 622 m  
**Elevation Loss:** 615 m  

**Technical Rating:** Advanced  
**Physical Rating:** Hard  
**Season:** June - October  
**Trail Type:** X-Country  

Jumpingpound Ridge is one of the very few classic alpine ridge rides located in Kananaskis Country. This fantastic trail may be ridden on its own, as an out-and-back, either direction, one way, or may be combined with several options to add to this already incredible ride. There are two main trailheads for Jumpingpound Ridge: north and south. The north trailhead is 7.5 km south of Dawson Recreational Area and the south trailhead is 17 km south from Dawson and 15 km north of Hwy 66 and the Elbow Falls Trail.

Jumpingpound Ridge south trailhead begins from the large and obvious Powderface Trail pull-off and heads east, crossing a short pedestrian bridge before beginning to climb. The climb up begins to head north and is a long switchbacking ascent with several steep sections, making this a tough slug to the top of the ridge. Near the top of the climb you will come across a junction for Jumpingpound Summit, heading west (left). Keep right and continue to climb up to the ridge. One more junction for Jumpingpound Mountain will greet you, less than 0.5 km before you reach the ridge. Stop to take in the views here, hike up the short section to Jumpingpound Mountain to check out the views, or continue on left to begin your ride along the ridge. Once you cross the ridge, you'll come to a junction for Cox Hill. Keep west (left) to head down to Powderface Trail, unless you're partaking in the Jumpingpound Ridge to Cox Hill ride. The last part of Jumpingpound Ridge trail is a fast switchbacking descent, with lots of roots and loose rock to keep things exciting. Once you finish the descent you'll cross the creek and spit out on to Powderface Trail. From there, return to your vehicle taking Powderface Trail, or hop in a retrieval vehicle you arranged before you began this ride.

**TRAILHEAD | N50 59.196 W114 57.338 (NORTH TH); N50 54.917 W114 55.078 (SOUTH TH)**

North TH: The north trailhead is located 7.5 km south of Dawson Recreational Area, on the east side of Powderface Trail.

South TH: The south trailhead is located on the east side of Powderface Trail, 100 m north of Canyon Creek, 17 km south of Dawson Recreation Area. Or 15 km north of Hwy 66 from the Elbow Falls Trail.

# 60 | JP SUMMIT TO JP RIDGE  LOOP | 💀💀💀💀💀

| | |
|---|---|
| Distance: 16 km | Technical Rating: Advanced |
| Time: 1.5 - 3 hrs | Physical Rating: Hard |
| Elevation Gain: 609 m | Season: June - October |
| Elevation Loss: 611 m | Trail Type: X-Country |

A shorter version of the classic Jumpingpound Ridge to Cox Hill Loop, the Jumpingpound Summit to Jumpingpound Ridge Loop is a slight alteration which leaves out the Cox Hill segment. It's possible to ride this loop after work during the summer months when daylight extends well into the evening. The shorter version of the original classic still offers some incredible riding, breathtaking scenery and spectacular singletrack climbs and descents. And don't forget about the sweet ridge ride along Jumpingpound Ridge. The whole loop shouldn't take more than 1.5 – 3 hours to complete, and even less if you set up a shuttle to avoid riding Powderface Trail.

There are several options to ride this loop.  You can do so clockwise or counter clockwise; you may also choose to set up a shuttle between the trailheads for Jumpingpound Ridge and Jumpingpound Summit if you would like to avoid riding the 6.2 km Powderface Trail connecting the two. My preference is to ride this fun loop counter clockwise. Drop your car at the Jumpingpound Ridge pull off, located on Powderface Trail, about 7.5 km south from the Dawson Recreational area. From there ride Powderface Trail for 6.2 km to the trailhead for Jumpingpound Summit. Sometimes hard to spot, the trail is located on the east side (left) of the road heading into the woods. It is marked with a map at the trailhead to help get the rider oriented. Pedal up the twisting, winding and switchbacking singletrack trail to where it meets with Jumpingpound Ridge. From there, take a left, heading north along Jumpingpound Ridge for the last bit of climbing before popping out of the woods. Continue left at the junction for Jumpingpound Mountain. The trail will pop out on Jumpingpound Ridge and continue along until the Cox Hill junction, at which point you will turn left (west) to descend the final leg of your ride, ending up at the Jumpingpound Ridge trailhead.

**TRAILHEAD | N50 56.335 W114 56.035 (JP SUMMIT); N50 59.196 W114 57.338 (JP RIDGE)**

From the Dawson Recreation Area, drive 7.5 km south on Powderface Trail, a dirt road, to reach the northern trailhead for Jumpingpound Ridge. Park or drop a retrieval vehicle here and continue another 6.2 km south to the Jumpingpound Summit trailhead where you will begin your ride. The trailhead is located on the east (left) side of the road; while well-marked, it is still hard to spot.

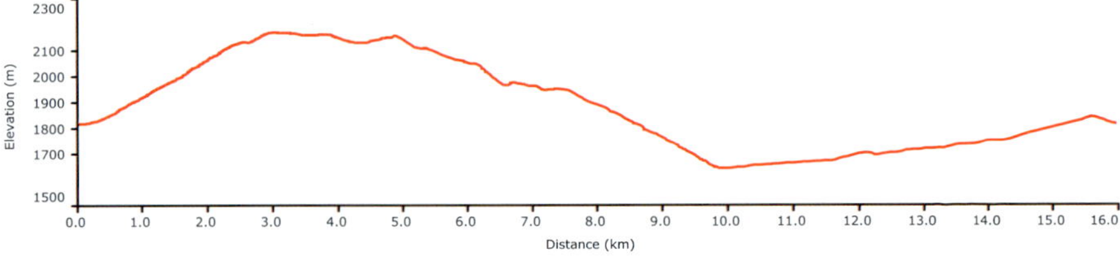

    *Find the Hidden Treasures: A Guide to Mountain Bike Trails in Kananaskis Country*

# 61 | JUMPINGPOUND RIDGE TO COX HILL | 

**Distance:** 18.5 km
**Time:** 3 – 5 hrs
**Elevation Gain:** 823 m
**Elevation Loss:** 1,061 m

**Technical Rating:** Advanced
**Physical Rating:** Hard
**Season:** July - September
**Trail Type:** X-Country

Jumpingpound Ridge Trail to Cox Hill Trail is an epic x-country ride with incredible 360 degree views of the surrounding mountains. Located in the Sibbald Area of Kananaskis Country, this ride has it all: loads of switchbacks, amazing singletrack, awesome alpine ridge riding and some incredible descents. This route may be ridden as a loop or as a half loop, when setting up a retrieval vehicle. To set up your retrieval, drop a vehicle at Dawson Recreational Area. Pile into a second vehicle and drive south on Powderface Trail about 17 km to the Jumpingpound Ridge south trailhead. Begin your ride up Jumpingpound Ridge Trail, returning to Dawson Recreational Area via Cox Hill Trail. Once back at Dawson, send your drivers back down to Jumpingpound Ridge south trailhead to retrieve your vehicle(s).

Jumpingpound Ridge is an incredible alpine ridge ride that starts with a long and steady climb, consisting of switchbacks and some gnarly technical sections. Once you reach the top of the climb, you will pop out of the woods and ride the ridge over to the start of the Cox Hill Trail heading right (north) at the well-marked junction. The start of Cox Hill begins with a short and fast descent before you begin climbing. A few steep and narrow switchbacks take you back up to the alpine. Follow the ridge to the summit of Cox Hill. Enjoy the scenery once you reach the summit; grab a lunch, hydrate, and get ready to start the fast and technical descent back down to the Dawson parking lot.

**TRAILHEAD | N50 54.915 W114 55.078 (TH); N51 01.387 W114 52.917 (DAWSON)**

Begin this ride by parking at Dawson Recreation Area and riding 17 km south along Powderface Trail to Jumpingpound Ridge south trailhead. From there take Jumpingpound Ridge north over to Cox Hill, returning to Dawson Recreational Area via Cox Hill Trail.

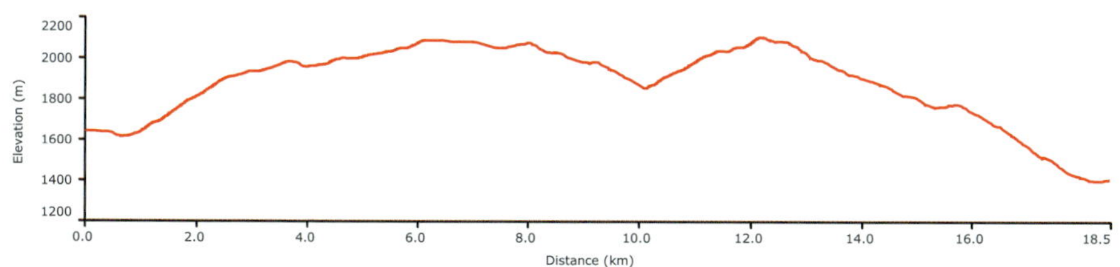

Cox Hill

Lusk Pass

bikepirate×com
MAP 7: ELBOW VALLEY
N
Evan-Thomas Day Use
40
40
Evan-Thomas Fire Road
2000
2438
2134
1829
2400
Prairie Creek Trail
Prairie Mountain
Prairie Link Trail
Powderface Creek Trail
Elbow Valley Trail
66
Powderface
to Bragg Creek / Calgary
66
Powderface Ridge Trail
Powderface Trail
Little Elbow Recreation Area
Mount Remus
Mount Romulus
Little Elbow Trail
Mount Glasgow
2743
Mount Cornwall
2438
Banded Peak
2743
Big Elbow Trail
Threepoint Mountain
Tombstone Mountain
Tombstone Campground
2800
2000
TransCanada Highway 1
Paved Road/Highway
Dirt Road
Trailhead
Water
1800 Height in metres (m)
Trail Junction
Beginner Trails
Intermediate Trails
Advanced / Expert Trails
Camping
Toilets / Outhouse
Parking
3 km
SCALE
bikepirate×com

# ELBOW VALLEY

Elbow Valley lies approximately 60 km west of Calgary and is accessed via Hwy 66. Hwy 66 runs west of Bragg Creek and ends at the Little Elbow Campground. Please note that the short section of Hwy 66 between Elbow Falls and Little Elbow Campground is closed to vehicles during December 1 – May 14.

Elbow Valley is a vast area with numerous classic trails open to mountain biking. Most trails combine long climbs up doubletrack trails, with several sections of singletrack to form some spectacular rides. High alpine rides along ridge tops, heading through incredible passes, are what the rider will find in this area. Suggested rides include Powderface Creek to Prairie Creek Loop and the Elbow Loop.

Elbow Loop

# 62 | ELBOW LOOP | 💀 💀 💀 💀

| | |
|---|---|
| Distance: 43 km | Technical Rating: Intermediate |
| Time: 3 - 6 hrs | Physical Rating: Hard |
| Elevation Gain: 862 m | Season: July - October |
| Elevation Loss: 850 m | Trail Type: X-Country |

Elbow Loop is a classic Rocky Mountains ride which combines the Big and Little Elbow trails into one full loop. The scenery on the mostly doubletrack (4WD) trail is breathtaking as it takes you through the Tombstone Pass. Pack your overnight gear and stay a night or two at the Tombstone Campground (camping permits are required) or take a side trip hike up to Tombstone Lakes; the trailhead is located about 15 km up Little Elbow Trail and no bikes are permitted on this side trip.

Elbow Loop may be ridden either direction, but the preferred route is counter-clock-wise. Starting up Little Elbow trail ride over to the forks and return via the Big Elbow trail ending at the suspension bridge crossing the Little Elbow River, returning you to the trailhead.

Expect a gradual gravel climb up Little Elbow all the way to Tombstone Pass before descending a short but fast section down to Big Elbow Valley. Make sure to turn left onto Big Elbow – there is a large sign indicating the turn – as heading right will take you down to the Tombstone Campground. After turning left onto Big Elbow, you will be greeted with a few short and steep climbs on more gravel roads, before the trail turns into some of the most amazing and breathtaking singletrack found on this ride. Following the flowy singletrack, the trail turns back to a wide gravel descent crossing a few creeks and the river along the way. The last part of trail on the Big Elbow takes you out along an open, yet flat, gravel doubletrack that follows the Elbow River before crossing the final suspension bridge back to the trailhead parking lot.

### TRAILHEAD | N50 47.659 W114 51.174 (PARKING); N50 47.346 W114 52.016 (LITTLE ELBOW); N50 47.464 W114 51.496 (BIG ELBOW)

Take Hwy 66 from Bragg Creek to Little Elbow Recreational Area. Parking is located near the suspension bridge; look for the trailhead sign indicating where to park. From the carpark ride through the campground west, to the start of the Little Elbow Trail, or start at the suspension bridge if riding clockwise on the Big Elbow trail.

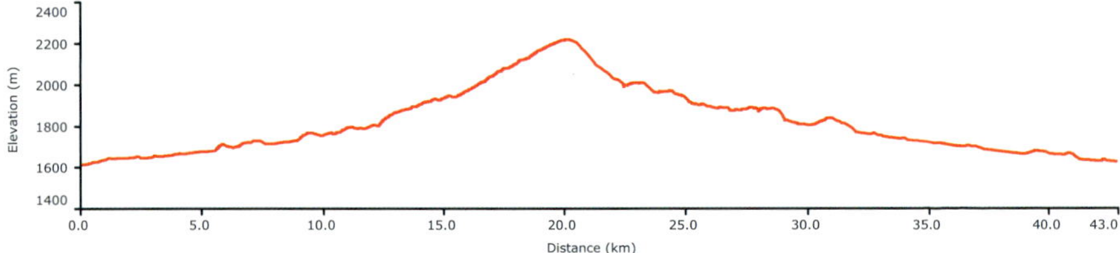

    *Find the Hidden Treasures: A Guide to Mountain Bike Trails in Kananaskis Country*

# 63 | POWDERFACE CREEK TO PRAIRIE CREEK LOOP | 

| | |
|---|---|
| Distance: 21 km | Technical Rating: Intermediate |
| Time: 2 - 4 hrs | Physical Rating: Moderate |
| Elevation Gain: 714 m | Season: June - October |
| Elevation Loss: 713 m | Trail Type: X-Country |

The following loop is an awesome ride located in the Elbow Valley. It combines the popular Powderface Creek Trail with Prairie Creek Trail to form a challenging mountain bike loop. Fantastic views at Powderface Pass and a few fast and technical singletrack descents following a number of switchbacks will greet the rider along this route.

The loop begins up Powderface Creek Trail and doesn't give the rider much time to warm up. A steep doubletrack climb right out of the parking lot will set the tone for the first part of this ride. After about 500 m the steep climb eases off and the rider is treated to some rolling terrain along the creek bed. At km 3 (junction) keep left unless you want to opt out for a shorter loop – referred to as the Powderface Creek to Prairie Link Loop. A long sustained climb will take you up to Powderface Pass from the 3 km mark. From there, it's smooth sailing down a technical singletrack to Powderface Trail, a gravel road. Take a right onto the gravel road and ride for 2.7 km to reach the final installment of this awesome ride – Prairie Creek trailhead. Turn right onto Prairie Creek and follow this flowy singletrack through tight trees, open meadows, and along a short ridge all the way back to the carpark.

**TRAILHEAD | N50 51.910 W114 47.528 (PARKING); N50 51.908 W114 47.551 (TH)**

Take Hwy 66 to Elbow Falls. Park at the Powderface carpark off of Hwy 66 west of Elbow Falls. The trailhead is located at the end of the parking lot.

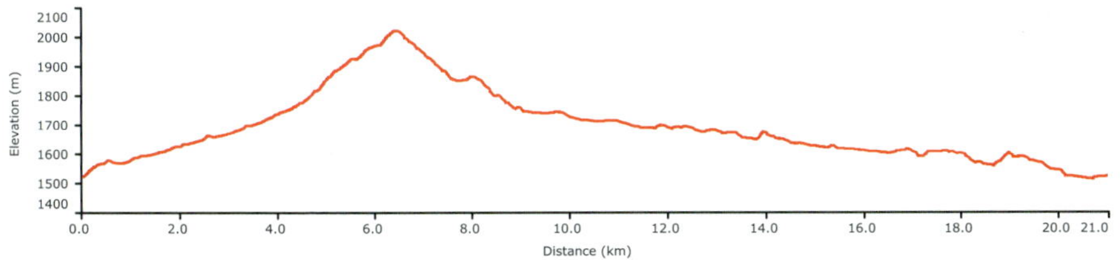

# 64 | POWDERFACE CREEK TO PRAIRIE LINK LOOP | 

Distance: 12 km
Time: 1.5 - 2 hrs
Elevation Gain: 373 m
Elevation Loss: 372 m

Technical Rating: Intermediate
Physical Rating: Moderate
Season: June - October
Trail Type: X-Country

Powderface Creek to Prairie Link Loop is a shorter version of the Powderface Creek to Prairie Creek Loop, located in Elbow Valley. It combines the best of Powderface Creek and Prairie Creek trails, leaving out the torturous rocky climb up to Powderface Ridge, adding a great new section to this shorter loop that may be completed after work during the long summer evenings.

Ride Powderface Creek to Prairie Link Loop clockwise or counter clockwise; the choice is yours. However, I find that this multi-use loop flows best when ridden clockwise. Begin the ride from Powderface parking lot up Powderface Creek Trail. The first section of trail begins with a steep 500 m incline most riders will find long enough to get their heart pounding and lungs gasping for air. Once this short, steep section is complete, the trail will continue to ascend at a more manageable grade all the way up to the Prairie Link turn-off, about 3 km from the parking area. Turn right (north) on to Prairie Link Trail and continue to climb up a narrow doubletrack through the thick forest, before descending down to Prairie Creek. Cross the well-constructed wooden bridge at the bottom of Prairie Link, turn right, and head east along the Prairie Creek Trail. The remainder of the trip is mostly down, as the trail descends along the creek. You will be greeted with one last technical climb near the end of the loop, which will provide some incredible views of the canyon and creek below. The last 2 km after that will descend back down towards Hwy 66, which you will pop out onto and ride southwest (right) for less than 200 m to the Powderface parking area.

## TRAILHEAD | N50 51.909 W114 47.561

From Calgary drive west along Hwy 22x, past the Bragg Creek turn-off. Hwy 22x turns into Hwy 66 at this point. Continue west along Hwy 66 until you reach Powderface parking area, on the north side of the Hwy across from Elbow Falls Recreational Area. Park and begin your ride up Powderface Creek Trail.

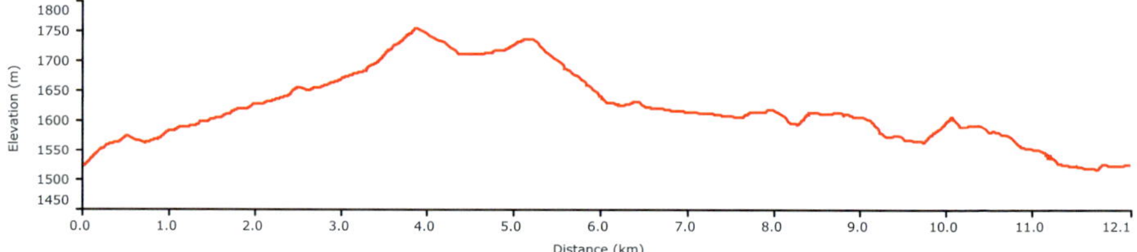

# 65 | POWDERFACE RIDGE TRAIL | ☠☠

Distance: 9.6 km
Time: 2 - 3 hrs
Elevation Gain: 663 m
Elevation Loss: 525 m

Technical Rating: Expert
Physical Rating: Extreme
Season: July - October
Trail Type: X-Country

Stop right there. Do not read any further if you don't enjoy suffering. This ride is intense! It starts with a steep rocky and rooty climb that is relentless for the first 2 km. If you like taking your bike for a walk, than this ride is for you. Expert riders will have a tough time clearing the first bit, a definite challenge. At the 4.6 km mark you will pop out of the woods atop Powderface Ridge. Here is where you're rewarded for all the hard work; amazing 360 degree views of the surrounding mountains await you. The trail splits at this junction; stay right (north) to meet up with Powderface Creek Trail and begin your descent left (west) to Powderface Trail, a dirt road. The fast, windy and switchbacking descent will keep you on your toes and provide some excitement as you cruise down to the dirt road. Near the bottom of the descent the trail splits again. Follow the marker right to enjoy more sweet singletrack instead of taking the whole shot out on the doubletrack trail to the road.

Powderface is a multi-use trail, frequented by equestrians and hikers; please give right of way to other users if you decide to take on this adventure. Ride it as a loop connecting to Powderface Trail, a dirt road, looping south (left) back to your vehicle. You may also loop it with Powderface Creek Trail or Prairie Creek Trail if you're looking to extend your ride. However, this option will involve some road riding along Hwy 66 to get back to your vehicle.

### TRAILHEAD | N50 48.309 W114 50.541

From Bragg Creek take Hwy 66 west to the junction with Powderface Trail, a dirt road. Park at the pull-out and proceed up the steep singletrack trail directly up from Powderface Trail. About 50 m up the trail there is a trailhead marker indicating you are on the right track.

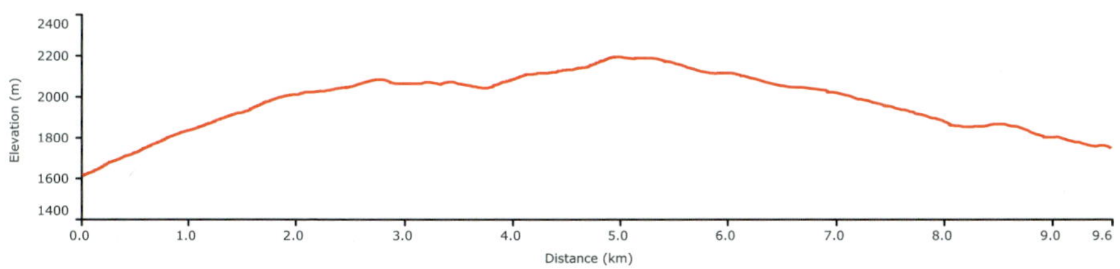

Prairie Creek Trail

MAP 8: BOW VALLEY PARK
N
Bow River
Bow Valley Campground
1X
Willow Rock Campground
Kananaskis River
Bow Valley Park Administration
Bow Valley Bike Path (Paved)
Stoney Trail
Chilver Lake
300 m
SCALE
TransCanada Highway 1
Paved Road/Highway
Dirt Road
Trailhead
Water
1800 Height in metres (m)
Trail Junction
Beginner Trails
Intermediate Trails
Advanced / Expert Trails
Camping
Toilets / Outhouse
Parking
bikepirate✕com
bikepirate✕com

# 66 | BOW VALLEY BIKE PATH | 

| | |
|---|---|
| Distance: 8.6 km (return) | Technical Rating: Beginner |
| Time: 30 min – 1 hr | Physical Rating: Easy |
| Elevation Gain: 85 m | Season: May - October |
| Elevation Loss: 85 m | Trail Type: Paved pathway |

Bow Valley Bike Path is a paved trail which runs from the administration and information centre building at the Bow Valley Provincial Park to the RV campground located in the park. The campsite is about 4.3 km west of the administration and information building. A tranquil and scenic path, the trail is great for those camping in the area and looking to get out on their bikes for a spin. It is a multi-use path, ridden as an out-and-back, so watch out for runners and walkers with burleys/strollers strolling along this trail.

The paved trail runs along gently rolling terrain surrounded by forest and meadows that open up with some great views. This is a great trail to be enjoyed with the kids.

## TRAILHEAD | N51 04.911 W115 03.850

Take Hwy 1 to exit Hwy 1X north (Bow Valley Provincial Park). Once on 1X take the first left (west) into the Bow Valley Provincial Park. Park at the administration and information building, 500 m from the 1X turn off. The east trailhead is well marked and starts from the administration and information building.

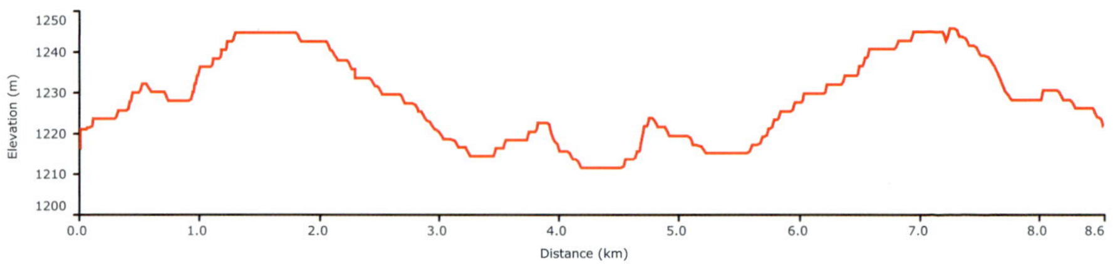

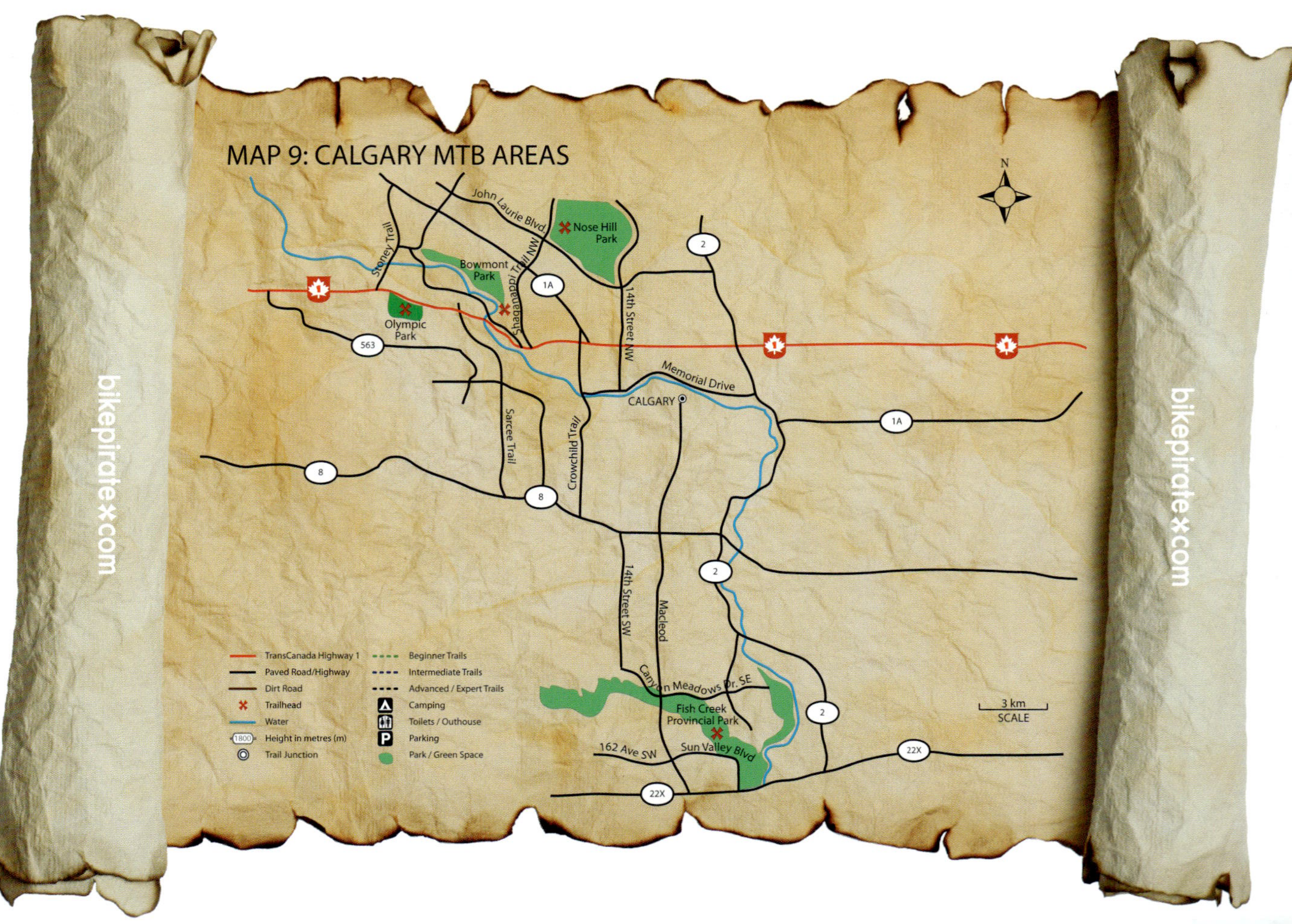

MAP 9: CALGARY MTB AREAS
N
bikepirate✴com
bikepirate✴com
John Laurie Blvd
Nose Hill Park
2
Stoney Trail
Bowmont Park
Shaganappi Trail NW
1A
14th Street NW
563
Olympic Park
Memorial Drive
CALGARY
1A
Sarcee Trail
Crowchild Trail
8
8
14th Street SW
Macleod
2
2
Canyon Meadows Dr. SE
Fish Creek Provincial Park
162 Ave SW
Sun Valley Blvd
2
22X
22X
22X
3 km
SCALE
TransCanada Highway 1
Paved Road/Highway
Dirt Road
Trailhead
Water
1800 Height in metres (m)
Trail Junction
Beginner Trails
Intermediate Trails
Advanced / Expert Trails
Camping
Toilets / Outhouse
Parking
Park / Green Space

# CALGARY AREA MOUNTAIN BIKE TRAILS

As a bonus, I've included in this book the three main riding areas found in Calgary for those riders new to the city and because of the requests I've received from bikepirate followers to do so. The three main riding areas for mountain bikers to explore include: Bowmont Park, Nose Hill, and Fish Creek. All three areas are park land, so please stay on designated trails for mountain biking and respect other trail users.

For those looking to get out on their downhill bike and would like to explore lift-access trails located in Calgary, I recommend visiting Canada Olympic Park (COP); located in the northwest of the city. The COP bike park is open during the summer months, providing lift-access to some really fun and flowy trails designed by Whistler's Gravity Logic. The bike park trails range from the beginner to the advanced rider.

MAP 9.1: BOWMONT PARK MTB TRAILS
N
1 km
SCALE
Nose Hill Drive NW
Bearspaw Dam Rd. NW
85th Street NW
Bow River
46th Avenue NW
Silver Springs Gate NW
Silver Springs
Varsity Estate Drive NW
53rd Street NW
Silver Springs Golf Course
40 th Ave. NW
Sideshow Bob
Bow River
Bowness Road NW
Bowness Road NW
Sarcee Trail NW
Bowness Road NW
Bow River
52nd Street
Home Rd.
52nd Street Access
bikepirate✖com
bikepirate✖com
TransCanada Highway 1
Paved Road/Highway
Dirt Road
Trailhead
Water
Height in metres (m)
1800
Trail Junction
Beginner Trails
Intermediate Trails
Advanced / Expert Trails
Paved Pathway
Camping
Toilets / Outhouse
Parking

# 67 | BOWMONT PARK MTB TRAILS | ☠ ☠ ☠

| | |
|---|---|
| Distance: 11 km (total) | Technical Rating: Beginner – Advanced |
| Time: 1 – 3 hrs | Physical Rating: Moderate |
| Elevation Gain: Not applicable | Season: April - October |
| Elevation Loss: Not applicable | Trail Type: X-Country |

Located in the northwest of the city, this area offers some great riding for locals looking to get out on some fun singletrack during the week. The singletrack trails follow the Bow River and in many instances hug the escarpment. A multi-use area, one can also expect paved lanes and wide doubletrack. Please be respectful of other trail users, as you are riding in a park.

To download a GPS track of a suggested loop, one of many options available when riding the park, please visit www.bikepirate.com. The loop incorporates Sideshow Bob, a popular trail in the area. Sideshow is a narrow singletrack trail that hugs the hillside of the escarpment and offers up a few exposed sections of trail not suitable for beginner riders or those with a fear of heights. The remainder of the trails in the area are mainly intermediate in technical rating and fun to cruise on. Refer to the map included to explore and loop several trails in the area.

## TRAILHEAD | N51 04.829 W114 09.953 (52ND STREET PARKING)

There are several access points to the park, so the choice on where to begin your ride is entirely up to you. I typically access this area via 52nd Street. Take Hwy 1 (16th Avenue) to Home Road. Turn North on to Home Road. Halfway up the hill turn left on to 52 Street NW, a one-way street. Free parking is located on your right hand side in the large carpark.

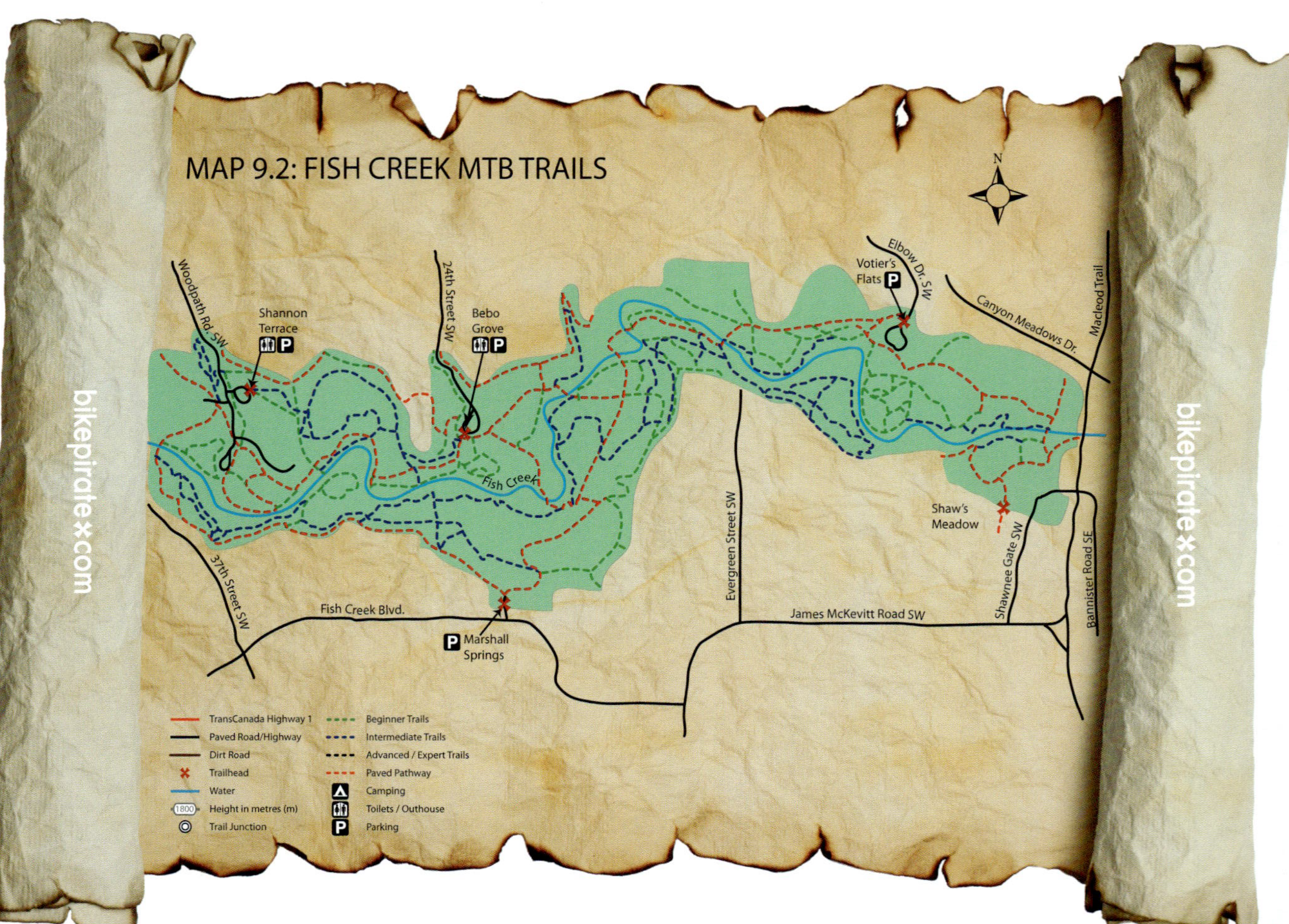
MAP 9.2: FISH CREEK MTB TRAILS
N
Woodpath Rd. SW
24th Street SW
Shannon Terrace
Bebo Grove
Elbow Dr. SW
Votier's Flats
Canyon Meadows Dr.
Macleod Trail
Fish Creek
37th Street SW
Fish Creek Blvd.
Marshall Springs
Evergreen Street SW
Shaw's Meadow
Shawnee Gate SW
James McKevitt Road SW
Bannister Road SE
bikepirate✕com
bikepirate✕com
TransCanada Highway 1
Paved Road/Highway
Dirt Road
Trailhead
Water
1800  Height in metres (m)
Trail Junction
Beginner Trails
Intermediate Trails
Advanced / Expert Trails
Paved Pathway
Camping
Toilets / Outhouse
Parking

# 68 | FISH CREEK MTB TRAILS | 💀💀

**Distance:** Over 40 km
**Time:** 1 - 4 hrs
**Elevation Gain:** Not applicable
**Elevation Loss:** Not applicable

**Technical Rating:** Beginner - Intermediate
**Physical Rating:** Easy
**Season:** May - October
**Trail Type:** X-Country

Fish Creek Provincial Park is located in the southwest of Calgary. It is one of North America's largest urban parks, boasting a hefty network of paved, granular and singletrack trails open to biking. The network of paved and granular paths connects the five main parking areas. A number of singletrack trails exist in this area and interlink the paved and granular paths. These trails are typically well marked; however, linking them to create a fun loop is another story. If you're looking to ride singletrack, then look to someone that knows the park well to help you get around.

The park is well suited to family outings and beginner riders. The paved and granular paths are easy to navigate with little elevation gain. Washroom facilities, fire pits, and picnic tables can be found at day use areas located in the park for your convenience and enjoyment.

Please remember to yield to hikers and dog walkers and note that all cycling is confined to designated trails; cycling is not permitted on pathways around Sikome Lake, nor is it permitted in front of Bow Valley Ranch Visitor Centre.

## TRAILHEAD | N50 55.322 W114 06.768 (MARSHALL SPRINGS)

There are five major parking areas in the western portion of the Park where a majority of the singletrack trail exists: Shannon Terrace, Bebo Grove, Votier's Flats, Glennfield and Marshall Springs. Refer to the overview map to access the day use area closest to you.

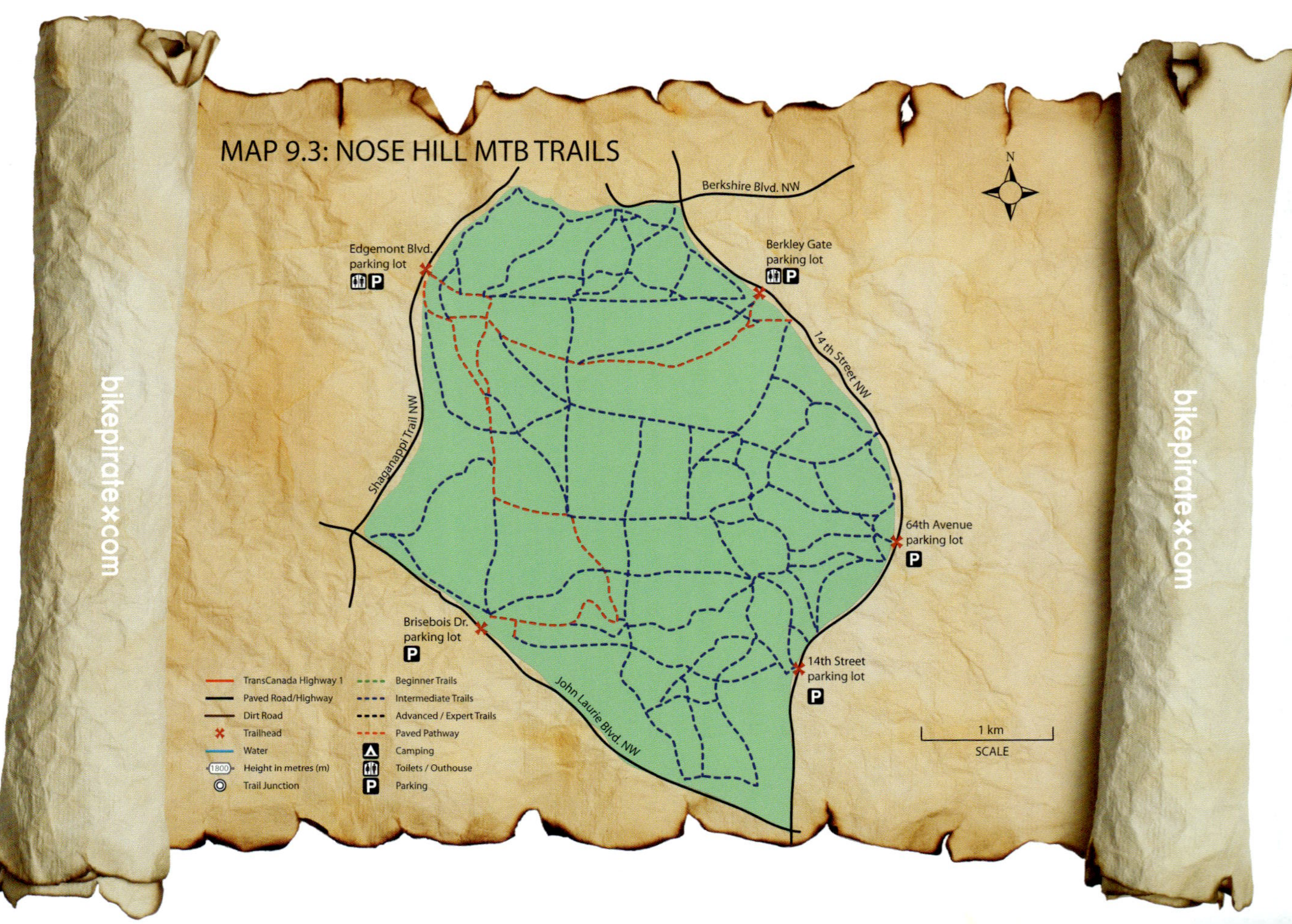

MAP 9.3: NOSE HILL MTB TRAILS
Berkshire Blvd. NW
Berkley Gate parking lot
Edgemont Blvd. parking lot
14 th Street NW
64th Avenue parking lot
14th Street parking lot
Brisebois Dr. parking lot
Shaganappi Trail NW
John Laurie Blvd. NW
1 km
SCALE
N
TransCanada Highway 1
Paved Road/Highway
Dirt Road
Trailhead
Water
Height in metres (m)
Trail Junction
Beginner Trails
Intermediate Trails
Advanced / Expert Trails
Paved Pathway
Camping
Toilets / Outhouse
Parking
1800
P

# 69 | NOSE HILL MTB TRAILS | 💀 💀

**Distance:** Over 18 km
**Time:** 1 – 3 hrs
**Elevation Gain:** Not applicable
**Elevation Loss:** Not applicable

**Technical Rating:** Beginner - Intermediate
**Physical Rating:** Easy
**Season:** May - October
**Trail Type:** X-Country

Located in northwest Calgary, Nose Hill Park covers 11.27 km² and is surrounded by 12 residential communities. The mountain bike trails range from beginner to intermediate. This is a great area for those learning to mountain bike wanting to get a taste of some smooth and rolling singletrack without much technical to throw you off your game. Nose Hill is a great early season ride as the trails do get overgrown during the summer months. Please stay on established trails when riding in this area.

There are a number of singletrack trails that zigzag and cross the main gravel and paved paths to explore. One can easily spend a few hours trying to link them all. A suggested beginner to intermediate loop is available for download for your GPS device at www.bikepirate.com. The 13.8 km loop will take anywhere from 1 – 2 hrs to complete.

## TRAILHEAD

Nose Hill is located in the northwest end of Calgary. There are six carparks located around Nose Hill Park providing access to the trails. The choice as to where to enter the park is completely up to you and based on where you reside. The map provided shows all main entrances and identifies the amenities at each.

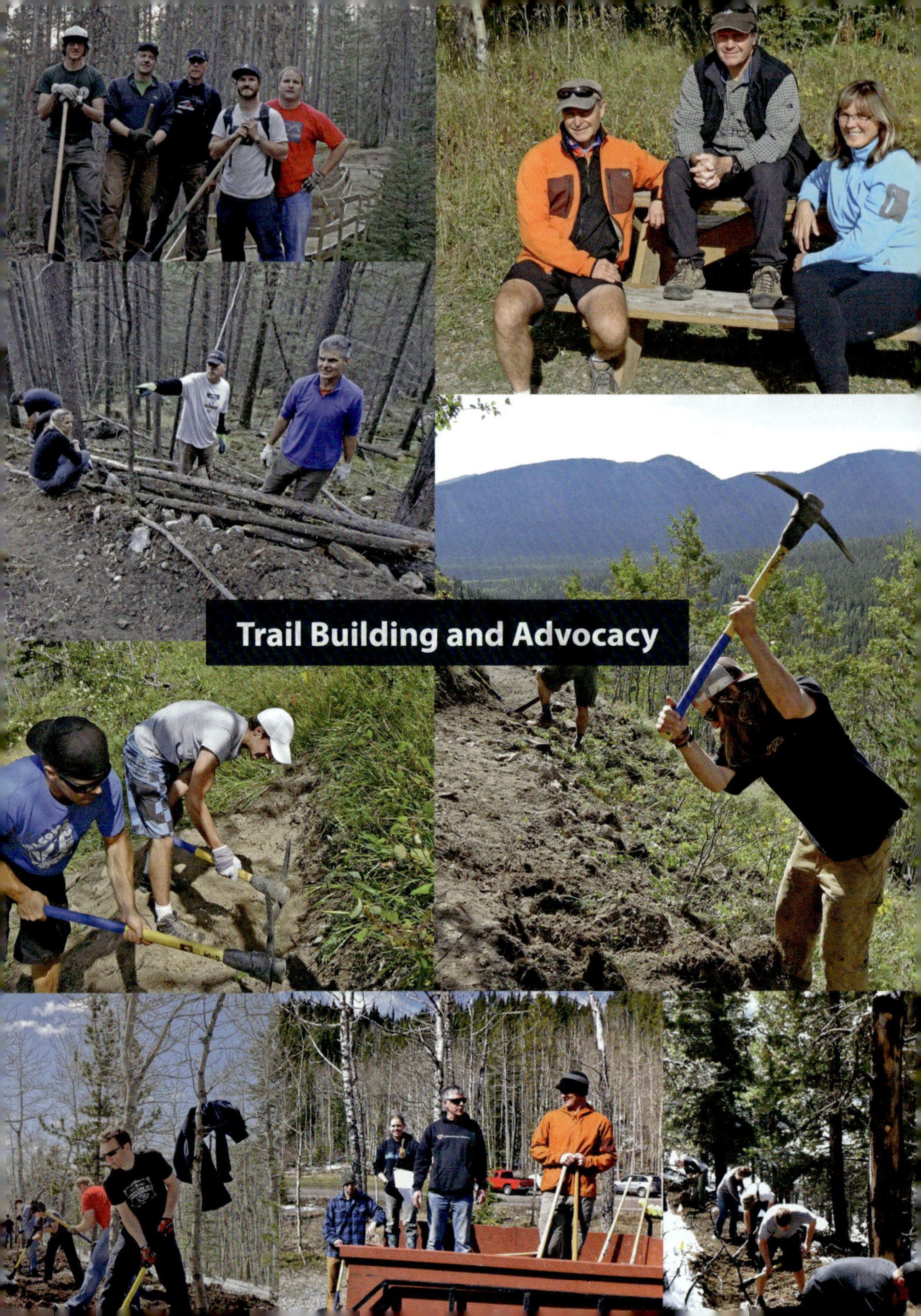
Trail Building and Advocacy

I once heard an acquaintance of mine speak at the 24 Hours of Adrenaline regarding trail building and maintenance. His opening line – "there are no trail fairies, trails don't build themselves" – struck a chord with me. Nicholas Dotchin, Program Manager for Friends of Kananaskis Country, was there to urge riders to get behind various volunteer efforts and put in some time to dig or donate and give back to help ensure the trails of today are here tomorrow for all of us to enjoy. This prompted me to add a section on trail advocacy organizations to this guidebook. My hope is that it will inform and educate riders and encourage them to do their part. Trails do not maintain themselves, nor do they magically appear as pointed out by Nic. It takes all our efforts to keep them in pristine shape. If all of us that ride did just one day of trail work per year, our trail system would not only get the love it deserves, but it would flourish. Think about it: what is one day a year worth to you?

The following advocacy groups, mainly made up of volunteers, several of whom I've come to know very well through my own volunteer efforts during trail days or via trail proposal submissions, are behind the efforts of creating, maintaining and lobbying for trails in Kananaskis Country. Without these dedicated individuals and organizations you wouldn't have the network of trails to ride that now exist in the area.

As a motto being adopted by several groups across the nation emphasizes: You ride, you dig!

## MOOSE MOUNTAIN BIKE TRAIL SOCIETY (MMBTS)

Formed in April of 2009 as an official not-for-profit organization, MMBTS is comprised of mountain bikers dedicated to the accessibility of trails and support of mountain biking in the Moose Mountain and surrounding area. This group of committed riders volunteer their time to oversee the trails located on Moose Mountain. They have done amazing work to upgrade the current trail system, build new trail and properly map and mark all existing trail. I LOVE their mission statement, especially the last bit, as I think it sums up mountain biking perfectly.

*Mission: To advocate, develop, and maintain mountain bike trails and to promote active, fun, environmentally responsible community involvement. Translation: To build, shred, and high-five.*

In the last few years we've seen the addition of several new trails on Moose, including SHAFT, Pneuma, Brakeless and Family Guy. Family Guy is a brand spanking new trail, which I hope will be completed by summer of 2013. Once complete, this trail will be the longest beginner/intermediate downhill ride on the west side of Moose Mountain. Many more projects are in the works and MMBTS needs your help to see these come to fruition. If you're a rider using the trails on Moose, consider volunteering, donating or buying a membership with MMBTS. For more information on how to get involved, contact: www.mmbts.com or info@mmbts.com.

## GREATER BRAGG CREEK TRAILS ASSOCIATION (GBCTA)

GBCTA is a purely volunteer group of Bragg Creek and area residents that are working hard to design, build and maintain trails and pathways for the benefit of residents and visitors to the Bragg Creek area. The group came into existence in 2004 and has done some incredible work in the West Bragg Creek area, building over 33 km of multi-use, all-season singletrack trails. The GBCTA efforts have truly paid off, clearly seen by increased visitation to the area during the summer. Trail users from Calgary and surrounding area now flock to these trails to experience the sweet, flowy singletrack conveniently located just outside the city limits.

What is truly unique about the GBCTA is that it's a collaboration of cyclists, hikers, horseback riders, x-country skiers, runners and snowshoers, all working together to build and maintain this incredible trail network. It's also the only place that I'm aware of to have such a unique approach to collaborative trail building, working with a large number of key user groups, including Alberta Tourism and Parks and Recreation, for the benefit of all.

A special mention goes out to Eric Lloyd, GBCTA Special Projects Coordinator. Eric raised over $285,000 to help make this multi-use, all-season trail network a reality. A local Bragg Creek resident and an avid x-country skier, hiker, and mountain biker, Eric and others envisioned an improved trail network for all- season use. Leading the charge for over three years, planning, fundraising and hiring the trail crew, Eric's efforts have finally started to pay off for all of us to enjoy. Thank you Eric!

With 25 km of planned trail yet to be built, the GBCTA is looking for volunteers and donations to help them maintain and expand the current network. For more information on how to get involved, contact: http://braggcreektrails.org/ or info@braggcreektrails.org.

## CALGARY MOUNTAIN BIKE ALLIANCE (CMBA)

Established in 1996, the CMBA is a not for profit organization dedicated to creating and improving multi-use non-paved trails in and around Calgary. They oversee the trails of Bowmont Park, Nose Hill and Fish Creek Provincial Park and were successful in securing $80,000 in public and private funding to build the Ridgeback trail; an 8 km of singletrack located in Kananaskis Country. Their efforts are far reaching, as can be seen by their recent work in West Bragg Creek. The CMBA partnered  with Greater Bragg Creek Trails Association in the design of the newly built West Bragg Creek singletrack trail network.

The CMBA is a great steward for the local trails, educating trail users, park delegates, and government bodies about mountain biking, sustainable trail development and access. Please consider lending this group your support by enrolling as a member, volunteering or donating. For more information on how to get involved contact: www.cmbalink.com or info@cmbalink.com.

## FRIENDS OF KANANASKIS COUNTRY

Friends of Kananaskis Country is a registered charity committed to sharing Kananaskis Country with the world through education, community engagement and volunteer participation.  Aligned with the Government of Alberta's vision of engaging the public in participating in the long-term use and enjoyment of Kananaskis Country, Friends is committed to assisting Alberta Parks, Kananaskis staff to build and maintain quality trails.

Each year Friends organizes many volunteer trail crews who spend countless hours working on the vast network of trails in Kananaskis Country.  Partnering with Alberta Parks and local trail groups, they support all recognized trails in the area. The Friends believe that education is an important element in all their volunteer projects and encourage learning and sharing amongst all participants.

If you like what this group does, please consider volunteering or donating to their cause. For more information, visit: www.kananaskis.org

## BOW VALLEY MOUNTAIN BIKE ALLIANCE (BVMBA)

BVMBA is an association of riders who reside in Canmore, Banff and Lake Louise. Alliance members work with land managers on general issues relating to mountain bike use, particularly in Banff National Park and the Canmore area. Many of these issues are related to environmental and wildlife concerns, as people and animals struggle to share the same physical space in the Bow Valley. Other work includes trail advocacy, education on sustainable use and maintenance of local trail systems. Trail maintenance is conducted throughout the year with help from volunteers; those wishing to get involved are encouraged to contact the BVMBA to help out.

Recently this group spearheaded the efforts to receive approval for Razors Edge, a newly built all-mountain trail near Canmore. The three-stage proposal was successful and once the required work on Razors Edge is complete, the trail should receive its official trail status, making it a sanctioned trail. The BVMBA will need your help in 2013 to complete the required trail work proposed, along with finishing up work on the newly built Banff trail. Please consider lending your support by volunteering or donating. For more information on how to get involved contact BVMBA at www.bvmba.org

## INTERNATIONAL MOUNTAIN BICYCLING ASSOCIATION (IMBA) CANADA

Although not directly involved in the local efforts, IMBA takes on a larger role across the nation, ensuring our trails are cared for and protected. Their mission is "to create, enhance, and preserve great trail experiences for mountain bikers across Canada". If you care about the trails you ride and want to see more mountain bike trails developed across our nation, please consider becoming an IMBA member. For more information, please visit: www.imbacanada.com

It should also be noted that aside from the fantastic work the above mentioned advocacy groups do on and off the trails in Kananaskis Country an interdisciplinary government group known as the **Kananaskis Trails Committee** is working to develop a sustainable recognized trails network through collaboration with local communities, stakeholders, volunteers and land managers. Those looking for more information about their mandate and processes, should visit: www.albertaparks.ca/kananaskis-country/park-research-management/kc-management/kananaskis-trails-committee.aspx

Almost three years ago I took a chance, a chance to follow my dream and build a content-based website aimed at providing accurate and complete information on places to mountain bike for riders of all abilities. The website is bikepirate.com. The trail information provided on bikepirate is uploaded by our team of riders, who either reside or travel to the areas we've documented to ensure the trail data is current, complete, and accurate. I love to ride my mountain bike and want to see more people partake in this awesome sport, whether they are new to riding or an experienced rider. My mission is to provide complete information – dirt – on places to ride, so that riders like you can make an informed decision on where to ride and in some cases where not to ride, and to help you find your hidden treasure.

In 2012 I wrote and self-published my first guidebook – Bow Valley Mountain Bike Trail Guide. With support from the local community, the book has done very well and continues to be a great resource for riders new to the area. My next installment is the book you hold in your hands today. I hope you find it a great resource and an exciting reference for places to ride in Kananaskis Country.

Since the launch of my new book, I have relocated to Whistler from my home in Canmore, where I spent the last six years exploring the surrounding trails. The move is a very exciting one, as it will allow me to expand the trail inventory listed on bikepirate.com. And let's not forget that it will allow me to ride virtually year round in nearby places, including the North Shore, the Sunshine Coast and Vancouver Island. However, I do plan to continue to take a few months off the bike each year to ski, another passion of mine.

What's next, you might ask? I hope to publish more guidebooks, launch a few apps and continue to grow the bikepirate brand so that the next time you're looking at exploring a new riding destination, you can look to bikepirate to find the latest dirt on places to ride.

Happy trails!

Peter Oprsal

PURE
cycle
South Calgary's
Bike Shop

MOUNTAIN | ROAD | KIDS
purecycle.ca | 403-201-4300

WHERE RUGGED PEAKS
MEET COZY SHEETS.

Buffalo Mountain Lodge - Banff, AB
Deer Lodge - Lake Louise, AB
Emerald Lake Lodge - Field, BC
Hotel Association of Canada's Green Key Eco-Rating Program
Canadian Rocky Mountain Resorts
True Mountain Lodging
800.661.1367 / crmr.com
CRMR

**bikepirate✱com**

Scan the QR code to visit the bikepirate **Trail Report** page for up-to-date information on current trail conditions, trail status and closures.

bikepirate.com/trail-report/